THE ETHICS OF BELIEF

AND OTHER ESSAYS

THE ETHICS OF BELIEF
AND OTHER ESSAYS

W. K. CLIFFORD
Introduction by Timothy J. Madigan

GREAT BOOKS IN PHILOSOPHY

 Prometheus Books

59 John Glenn Drive
Amherst, New York 14228-2197

Published 1999 by Prometheus Books
59 John Glenn Drive, Amherst, New York 14228–2197,
716–691–0133, ext. 207. FAX: 716–564–2711.
WWW.PROMETHEUSBOOKS.COM

03 02 01 00 99   5 4 3 2 1

Library of Congress Cataloging-in-Publication Data

Clifford, William Kingdon, 1845–1879
     The ethics of belief and other essays / W.K. Clifford ; introduction by
Timothy J. Madigan.
          p.   cm. — (Great books in philosophy)
     Originally published: London : Watts & Co., 1947.
     ISBN 1–57392–691–4 (paper : alk. paper)
     1. Ethics, Evolutionary. 2. Belief and doubt. I. Title. II. Series
BJ1311.C57   1999
170—dc21   98–52479
                                                                          CIP

Printed in the United States of America on acid-free paper

Additional Titles on the Philosophy of Religion in Prometheus's Great Books in Philosophy Series

See the back of this volume for a complete list of titles in Prometheus's Great Books in Philosophy and Great Minds series.

Contents

Introduction

Timothy J. Madigan

"It is wrong always, everywhere, and for anyone, to believe anything upon insufficient evidence." So wrote William Kingdon Clifford (1845–1879) in his famous essay "The Ethics of Belief" (1876). Clifford was 31 years old when he delivered this lecture to the exclusive debating group called the Metaphysical Society, which met in London nine times a year to discuss issues pertaining to philosophical ideas and religious beliefs. The members included some of the most notable figures of Victorian Society, such as William Gladstone, Thomas Henry Huxley, Archbishop Henry Manning, John Ruskin, and Alfred Lord Tennyson. Clifford, who was at the time Professor of Applied Mathematics at University College, London, found attending the Society's meetings and participating in its often heated debates to be one of the chief pleasures of his life.

"The Ethics of Belief" remains Clifford's best known work. Published in early 1877 in the *Contemporary Review*, one of the most popular journals in England, it drew an immediate response from critics, who took umbrage with Clifford's forthright—and rather pugnacious—attack on beliefs which, while giving comfort, have no solid support in fact. William James was to use "The Ethics of Belief" as the focal point of his own celebrated essay "The Will to Believe", in which he compared Clifford to a general who marshals his troops instead of sending them into battle for fear they will be killed. This was unfair to Clifford, who recognized that working hypotheses and assumptions are a necessary part of belief-formation. His quarrel was with considering such tentative propositions to be proper beliefs, worthy of knowledge claims. In turn, Clifford would have been strongly critical of James' defense of the right to believe in the existence of God when the empirical evidence for or against such a belief was equally insufficient. But by the time James wrote his essay (1890) Clifford was long dead.

"The Ethics of Belief" has often been anthologized, but usually in shortened form, and often without an adequate introduction to the thinker or his influences. The complete version is found in this volume. In addition to this particular essay, Clifford also made important contributions to the fields of mathematics, philosophy, and psychology. In the field of geometry, he helped to popularize the non-Euclidean geometries that had been discovered earlier in the nineteenth century. His writings on the possible biological basis of morality in many ways anticipated the field of evolutionary ethics. And he was an active participant in the discussion of what areas the newly-founded field of psychology should study.

William Kingdon Clifford was born in Exeter, England, on May 4, 1845. Not much is known about his early years. His father was a bookseller, dealing largely in devotional material, and served for a time as a justice of the peace. Clifford's mother, whose maiden name was Kingdon, died when he was only nine. He inherited from her a constitutional weakness which perhaps contributed to his early death from tuberculosis.

A precocious child, Clifford was educated at a small local school until the age of 15, when he was sent to King's College, London. Here, he began to reveal abilities not only in his chosen profession of mathematics, but also in the fields of literature and classics. In October 1863 he went to Trinity College, Cambridge, after winning a scholarship to attend there. Percival Frost, his tutor at Cambridge, was so impressed by Clifford's original work in geometry that he predicted the young man would gain a place among the leaders of science.

Whatever tasks Clifford set himself to, he persevered until he had mastered them. He learned French, German and Spanish because he thought these languages would be important to his work in mathematics; he also learned Arabic, Greek and Sanskrit because they were a challenge; hieroglyphics because it was a riddle; and even Morse code and shorthand, because he claimed to be interested in all methods of conveying thought. His enthusiasm for learning occurred fortuitously during the latter half of the nineteenth century, which was a time of tremendous innovations in such fields as astronomy, biology, chemistry, mathematics and philosophy—all areas which Clifford would both write in and lecture about.

Although slight in build, Clifford prided himself on his physical strength. His class yearbook gave him the accolade of being "one of the most daring athletes of the University." His proudest feat, taken on a dare, was to hang by his toes from the cross bars of a church tower's weathercock—one of the last times he was to find himself near a church of any sort.

Clifford had been an ardent Anglican in his early years, but underwent an experience several other devout men and women grappled with in the so-called "Victorian Crisis of Belief": a loss of faith in the historical accuracy and present relevance of the teachings of Christianity, especially the tenets of the official Anglican religion. But for Clifford, unlike many others, this was a *positive* experience, not a cause of despair. He saw knowledge in terms of adaptability. As new information became available, humans could learn more about how the universe really works, as opposed to relying upon the patchwork beliefs which religious institutions offered as truth. Just as the Greek and Roman civilizations had overcome their reliance upon Zeus and Jupiter, so the modern world could overcome its reliance on Jehovah. In a symposium he took part in entitled "The Influence Upon Morality of a Decline in Religious Belief" (the final essay of this volume), Clifford was the *only* writer among a dozen participants who did not predict that a moral decline would accompany the loss of comforting supernatural beliefs.

While at Cambridge, Clifford had been asked to join the Apostles, a secretive club of the twelve most outstanding students. Deep in the study of Aquinas at the time, he at first reveled in supporting Catholic doctrines. But the impact of evolutionary theory, which had been hotly debated since the publication of Charles Darwin's *On the Origin of Species* (1859), altered his views, as did his reading the moral writings of Herbert Spencer. Clifford no longer felt it necessary to explain scientific discoveries through the prism of existing religious dogmas. In fact, he came to see clerical institutions as the chief obstacles to scientific and moral advancement.

Clifford saw the relevance of applying the theory of evolution to human cultural development well before most scientists—including Charles Darwin himself—would have been comfortable in doing so. Clifford soon came to the conclusion that the Christian religion, be it High or Low church, was an impediment to human intellectual and social growth. He saw clearly that the chief opposition to Darwinian evolutionary theory was coming from the pulpits, and he allied himself with Thomas H. Huxley, the biologist popularly known as "Darwin's Bulldog."

In 1868 Clifford was elected to a fellowship at Trinity College, Cambridge. During this time, he continued to couple his academic pursuits with membership in debating societies that sharpened his wits. He was, for instance, a member of the Grote Club, which included other members who would make their mark on English society, including the economist Alfred Marshall, the philosopher Henry Sidgwick, and the logician John Venn. Marshall became a great friend of Clifford's, although he felt that Clifford was "too fond of astonishing people."

Clifford was one of the first English mathematicians to become interested in the work on non-Euclidean geometry that had been done by Riemann and Lobachevski, going so far as to translate the former's work and publish it in the influential journal *Nature.* His knowledge of languages, especially German, gave him the facility, which many of his colleagues lacked, to understand these foreign arguments, and his natural curiosity and willingness to follow such arguments to their logical conclusions made him receptive to the shocking implications of these mathematical works. The introduction of non-Euclidean geometry was not only a challenge to mathematicians in particular, but a blow in general to those philosophers and theologians who held to the existence of necessary and universal truths. If even Euclid's axioms could be questioned, after thousands of years of being unquestioned, then what *else* might prove assailable? The first essay published in this volume, "The Aims and Instruments of Scientific Thought", was a lecture he delivered before the members of the British Association in 1872. In it, he defends geometry as an experimental science—a point-of-view very much at odds with the prevailing opinion of the time. Clifford was never afraid to question any shibboleth, even those from his own profession.

Clifford continued to write important mathematical papers, at the rate of three or four a year, while keeping up his membership in various social and fraternal organizations, as well as continuing his public lectures. With his unique combination of scientific understanding and rhetorical persuasive skills, he was well suited for the latter pursuit. His obvious enthusiasm, and his desire to enlighten, as well as his great clarity, won over his audiences, even when his lectures dealt with the most abstruse topics in mathematics. Clifford gave most of his public lectures with only a few short notes as reference, revising them afterwards for publication. He spoke on such topics as the nature of atoms, the relationship of the eye to the brain, the conditions of mental development, and the composition of the sun, as well as the talks reprinted here on ethics and religion.

In 1870, Clifford demonstrated his more empirical interest in science by joining an eclipse expedition, which sailed to the Mediterranean. He fell in love with the area, even though his ship struck a rock near Catania, Italy and was sunk. It is interesting to note that a ship disaster was used as an illustrative point to begin his famous essay, "The Ethics of Belief", written six years later. He knew from experience what he was talking about.

In 1871, Clifford was appointed to the Professorship in

Applied Mathematics at University College, London, where he would spend the remainder of his short career. It was a congenial place for a freethinker like himself, since it was founded in 1827 to be a strictly secular institution, where professors would be free from having to swear allegiance to any religious oath.

One of the extracurricular activities Clifford became involved with at this time was psychical research. However, unlike many of his fellow professors, he was not taken in by so-called spirit mediums. In fact, he became a fierce advocate of the view that there was no such thing as disembodied consciousness, and he delighted in debunking paranormal claims. The field of psychology was just being formed, and it was still unclear what its perimeters would be. Clifford made it a special point to show how supposed psychics were guilty of using trickery of the basest sort to fool not only credulous believers but also learned professors. In addition, he argued that psychology's proper study was the physical brain and how it worked, *not* disembodied elements like ghosts. That was better left for children's nursery stories.

While his extracurricular affairs kept him busy, Clifford did not shirk from his professional duties at the university. Although he was punctilious about meeting all his academic obligations, on one occasion he did take a voluntary leave of absence from his scheduled lecture, informing his students that he would be absent on important business which would probably not occur again. The occasion was his marriage, on April 7, 1875, to Lucy Lane. The couple was to have two daughters, and it was by all accounts a happy marriage. Lucy outlived her husband by half a century, and she became in her own right a well-known novelist and dramatist.

It is a sad fact that Clifford, who devised a series of lesson plans to, as he put it, "help kids find out things for themselves" did not live long enough to educate his own daughters. He had a great fondness for children. He wrote fairy tales and nonsense verse, and delighted in putting on children's parties, where his laughter was as little constrained as that of the young ones he entertained.

In June 1874, Clifford was elected as a Fellow of the Royal Society, one of the highest scholarly honors in the United Kingdom. He had previously turned down the offer, with the remark that he did not want to be respectable just yet. Shortly thereafter, he was elected to the Metaphysical Society, the youngest member so chosen. The Society's discussions, which were primarily concerned with arguments for or against the rationality of religious belief, were of the highest caliber. For Clifford, the exercising of intellectual abilities in the company of fellow critical thinkers (whether they shared the same conclusions or not) was an opportunity not to be missed, and he attended as many sessions as he could, often regaling Lucy upon his return home with a near-verbatim report of the evening's proceedings.

In the spring of 1876, shortly after delivering "The Ethics of Belief" to the Metaphysical Society, the symptoms of lung disease began to manifest themselves. At first, Clifford attempted to ignore these signs. He continued his breakneck schedule of teaching classes, writing scholarly articles on mathematics and popular essays on public issues, as well as delivering public lectures, attending society meetings, and raising a family. It was only with great reluctance that he finally faced up to the fact of his own illness, and agreed to take six months' leave of absence in his beloved Mediterranean. Clifford returned to England in late 1876, but from that point on he confined his extracurricular activities primarily to writing reviews. Even so, he continued to tax his system, often writing late into the night, completing a long review entitled "Virchow on the Teaching of Science" in a single sitting.

One of the last projects Clifford worked on was especially near and dear to his heart. After discussions with Huxley, he came to the conclusion that a gathering of freethinkers from around the world should be held, the aim of which would be to liberate the peoples of all classes from degrading dogmas. Combining his republican sentiments with his scientific advocacy, Clifford was the driving force behind the Congress of Liberal Thinkers, which was held on June 13–14, 1878 at the South Place Chapel in England, just a few days after the commemoration of the centenary of Voltaire's death (May 30, 1778). Over 400 delegates came from throughout the United Kingdom and other European countries, as well as from India and the United States. The aims of the Congress were defined as:

1.The scientific study of religious phenomena. 2. The collection and diffusion of information concerning movements throughout the world. 3. The emancipation of mankind from the spirit of superstition. 4. Fellowship among liberal thinkers of all races. 5. The promotion of the culture, progress, and moral welfare of mankind, and of whatever in any form may tend towards that end. 6. Membership in this Association shall leave each individual responsible for his own opinion alone, and in no degree affect his relations with other associations.

The presidency of the association was conferred on Professor Huxley, who sadly noted that its leading figure, who had done more than anyone else to organize such a gathering of iconoclasts, and who was to have been the keynote speaker, was not present. Clifford's health had again collapsed, and he and Lucy had once again set sail for the Mediterranean. He tried to prepare a speech to be read in his absence, but even this proved too much a strain. He was able to send some brief remarks, which were read to the delegates, and which showed that his views remained as uncompromising as ever:

> Catholics are fond of saying that an age of atheism is approaching, in which we shall throw over all moral obligations, and society will go to ruin. Then we shall see what is the true effect of all our liberal and scientific teaching. As a matter of fact, however, even they themselves admit that the public conscience is growing in strength and straightness, while the Catholic dogmas and organism are more and more repudiated. We may see reason to believe that the former of those facts is the cause of the latter. Part of modern unbelief is no doubt due to the wider knowledge of criticism of the so-called "evidence of Christianity," but in all ages sensible men have seen through that flimsy structure. Intellectual scepticism is not really more rife than it has been in many past periods. The main ground of hope for the masses is the moral basis of scepticism—1. Its revolt against mythology; 2. Its revolt against the priestly organisation of the churches.

Clifford returned to England in August 1878, looking haggard and still enfeebled by the tuberculosis that was killing him. Friends noted that his spirits had not left him, but he was no longer capable of any but the simplest exertions. When made aware of a newspaper report which claimed that he was converting back to Christianity in his final days, Clifford fired back a retort that, while his doctor had certified that he was ill, "'twas not mental derangement." Huxley, who was a regular visitor to the Clifford home during these final days, lamented to friends that "the finest scientific mind in England for fifty years is dying in that house."

While travel was dangerous, it became evident as the winter weather ensued that Clifford's only hope for survival was to leave England and once again venture to a warmer climate. He and Lucy set sail for Madeira, Portugal, in February 1879. To its credit, the Senate of University College, London recommended that he keep his chair in Applied Mathematics, and his friends established a trust fund to help him and his family. Among the signatories of the fund were T. H. Huxley, Dr. William Spottiswood, president of the Royal Society, the mathematician H. J. S. Smith (who wrote an introduction for the posthumous collection of Clifford's mathematical papers), and Leslie Stephen and Sir Frederick Pollock (fellow members of the Metaphysical Society, who would co-edit the posthumous collection of Clifford's popular lectures and essays). Stephen, the father of future novelist Virginia Woolf and a noted philosopher and editor in his own right, would later write Clifford's biography, as well as continue to look after Clifford's family.

Clifford gave careful directions for the disposal of his papers. He had a long-standing interest in the life and work of Baruch Spinoza (in 1877 he had planned to lecture on this topic, but his health had not allowed it), so it is not surprising that Spinoza's great saying was often on Clifford's lips during this time: *Homo liber de nulla re minus quam de morte cogitat* ("There is nothing over which a free man ponders less than death").

William Kingdon Clifford died on March 3, 1879, at the

age of 33. His body was brought back from Madeira and buried in Highgate Cemetery, with an epitaph chosen from Epictetus: "I was not, and was conceived; I loved, and did a little work; I am not, and grieve not." Perhaps the most fitting written memorial for Clifford could be found in a letter he himself wrote to Lucy in 1874 during their courtship. It expresses quite nicely the type of person Clifford admired and wished to emulate, and symbolically represents his oft-stated goal of helping humanity to advance from the worship of Christ to the appreciation of the possibilities inherent in the human species itself:

> . . . there is room for some earnest person to go and preach around in a simple way the main straightforward rules that society has unconsciously worked out and that are floating in the air; to do as well as possible what one can do best; to work for the improvement of the social organisation; to seek earnestly after truth and only to accept provisionally opinions one has not inquired into; to regard men as comrades in work and their freedom as a sacred thing; in fact, to recognise the enormous and fearful difference between truth and falsehood, right and wrong, and how truth and right are to be got at by free inquiry and the love of our comrades for their own sakes and nobody else's.

It is fitting that this selection of Clifford's popular essays on ethics and religion (which have long been out-of-print) should again be published. One must read the following pieces with a critical eye, keeping in mind Clifford's own commitment to rational discourse. He fully expected his more outrageous assertions to be questioned. No one welcomed the give-and-take of public debate more than Clifford did. He wished to motivate all members of society to utilize their intellectual abilities to the highest degree. The following provocative and enlightening essays—all vintage Clifford—do just that.

—Timothy J. Madigan
Free Inquiry

FURTHER READINGS

Works by W. K. Clifford

The Common Sense of the Exact Sciences. Edited by Karl Pearson, with an introduction by James R. Newman and a preface by Bertrand Russell. New York: Alfred A. Knopf, 1946.

Lectures and Essays, Volumes I and II. Edited by Leslie Stephen and Frederick Pollock, with an introduction by Frederick Pollock. London: Macmillan, 1879.

Mathematical Papers. Edited by Robert Tucker, with an introduction by H. J. S. Smith. London: Macmillan, 1882.

Seeing and Thinking. London: Macmillan, 1879.

Works about W. K. Clifford and "The Ethics of Belief"

Berman, David. *A History of Atheism in Great Britain: From Hobbes to Russell.* London: Routledge, 1988.

Brown, Alan Willard. *The Metaphysical Society: Victorian Minds in Crisis, 1869–1880.* New York: Octagon Books, 1973.

Code, Lorraine. *Epistemic Responsibility.* Hanover: University of New England, 1987.

Farber, Lawrence Paul. *The Temptations of Evolutionary Ethics.* Berkeley: University of California Press, 1998.

Haack, Susan. " 'The Ethics of Belief' Reconsidered" in *The Philoso-*

phy of Roderick M. Chisholm. Chicago: Open Court Press, 1997: 129–144.

Hollinger, David A. "James, Clifford, and the Scientific Conscience" in The Cambridge Companion to William James, edited by Ruth Anna Putnam. New York: Cambridge University Press, 1997: 69–83.

Levine, George. "Scientific Discourse as an Alternative to Faith" in Victorian Faith in Crisis: Essays on Continuity and Change in Nineteenth-Century Religious Belief, edited by Richard J. Helmstadter and Bernard Lightman. Stanford: Stanford University Press, 1990: 225–261.

Lightman, Bernard. The Origins of Agnosticism: Victorian Unbelief and the Limits of Knowledge. Baltimore: Johns Hopkins University Press, 1987.

Madigan, Timothy J. "Ethics and Evidentialism: W. K. Clifford and 'The Ethics of Belief.' " In The Journal for the Critical Study of Religion, Ethics, and Society, Volume 2, Number 1 (Spring/Summer 1997): 9–18.

Madigan, Timothy J. "Verily, He Died Too Young: A Comparison of Friedrich Nietzsche and W. K. Clifford" in The New Zealand Rationalist and Humanist (Spring 1998): 2–7.

McCarthy, Gerald D., ed. The Ethics of Belief Debate. Atlanta: Scholars Press, 1986.

Pyle, Andrew, ed. Agnosticism: Contemporary Responses to Spencer and Huxley. London: Thoemmes Press, 1995.

Rorty, Richard. "Religious Faith, Intellectual Responsibility, and Romance" in The Cambridge Companion to William James, edited by Ruth Anna Putnam. New York: Cambridge University Press, 1997: 84–102.

Quinton, Anthony. "On the Ethics of Belief" in From Wodehouse to Wittgenstein. New York: St. Martin's Press, 1998: 78–96.

ON THE AIMS AND INSTRUMENTS OF SCIENTIFIC THOUGHT [1]

IT may have occurred (and very naturally too) to such as have had the curiosity to read the title of this lecture, that it must necessarily be a very dry and difficult subject; interesting to very few, intelligible to still fewer, and, above all, utterly incapable of adequate treatment within the limits of a discourse like this. It is quite true that a complete setting-forth of my subject would require a comprehensive treatise on logic, with incidental discussion of the main questions of metaphysics; that it would deal with ideas demanding close study for their apprehension, and investigations requiring a peculiar taste to relish them. It is not my intention now to present you with such a treatise.

The British Association, like the world in general, contains three classes of persons. In the first place, it contains scientific thinkers; that is to say, persons whose thoughts have very frequently the characters which I shall presently describe. Secondly, it contains persons who are engaged in work upon what are called scientific subjects, but who in general do not, and are not expected to, think about these subjects in a scientific manner. Lastly, it contains persons who suppose that their work and their thoughts are unscientific, but who would like to know something about the business of the other two classes aforesaid. Now, to anyone who belonging to one of these classes considers either of the other two, it will be apparent that there is a certain gulf between him and them; that he does not quite understand them, nor they him; and that an opportunity for sympathy and comradeship is lost through this want of understanding. It is this gulf that I desire to bridge over, to the best of my power. That the scientific thinker may consider his business in relation to the great life of mankind; that the noble army of practical workers may recognise their fellowship with the outer world, and the spirit which must guide both; that this so-called outer world may see in the work of science only the putting in evidence of all that is excellent in its own work—may feel that the kingdom of science is within it: these are the objects of the present discourse. And they compel me to choose such portions of my vast subject as shall be intelligible to all, while they ought at least to command an interest universal, personal, and profound.

In the first place, then, what is meant by scientific thought? You may have heard some of it expressed in the various Sections this morning. You have probably also heard expressed in the same places a great deal of unscientific thought; notwithstanding that it was about mechanical energy, or about hydrocarbons, or about eocene deposits, or about malacopterygii. For scientific thought does not mean thought about scientific subjects with long names. There are no scientific subjects. The subject of science is the human universe; that is to say, everything that is, or has been, or may be related to man. Let us then, taking several topics in succession, endeavour to make out in what cases thought about them is scientific, and in what cases not.

Ancient astronomers observed that the relative motions of the sun and moon recurred all over again in the same order about every nineteen years. They were thus enabled to predict the time at which eclipses would take place. A calculator at one of our observatories can do a great deal more than this. Like them, he makes use of past experience to predict the future; but he knows of a great number of other cycles besides that one of the nineteen years, and takes account of all of them; and he can tell about the solar eclipse of six years hence exactly when it will be visible, and how much of the sun's surface will be covered at each place, and, to a second, at what time of day it will begin and finish there. This prediction involves technical skill of the highest order; but it does not involve scientific thought, as any astronomer will tell you.

By such calculations the places of the planet Uranus at different times of the year had been predicted and set down. The predictions were not fulfilled. Then arose Adams, and from these errors in the prediction he calculated the place of an entirely new planet, that had never yet been suspected; and you all know how the new planet was actually found in that place. Now this prediction does involve scientific thought, as anyone who has studied it will tell you.

Here then are two cases of thought about the same subject, both predicting events by the application of previous experience, yet we say one is *technical* and the other *scientific*.

Now let us take an example from the building of bridges and roofs. When an opening is to be spanned over by a material construction, which must bear a certain weight without bending enough to injure itself, there are two forms in which this construction can be made, the arch and the chain. Every part of an arch is compressed or pushed by the other parts; every part of a chain is in a state of tension, or is pulled by the other parts. In many cases these forms are united. A girder consists of two main pieces or booms, of which the upper one acts as an arch and is compressed, while the lower one acts as a chain and is pulled; and this is true even when both the pieces are quite straight. They are enabled to act in this way by being tied together, or braced, as it is called, by cross pieces, which you must often have seen. Now suppose that any good practical engineer makes a bridge or roof upon some approved pattern which has been made before. He designs the size and shape of it to suit the opening which has to be spanned; selects his material according to the locality; assigns the strength which must be given to the several parts of the structure according to the load which it will have to bear. There is a great deal of thought in the making of this design, whose success is predicted by the application of previous experience; it requires technical skill of a very high order; but it is not scientific thought. On the other hand, Mr. Fleeming Jenkin [1] designs a roof consisting of two arches braced together, instead of an arch and a chain braced together; and although this form is quite different from any known structure, yet before it is built he assigns with accuracy the amount of material that must be put into every part of the structure in order to make it bear the required load, and this prediction may be trusted with perfect security. What is the natural comment on this? Why, that Mr. Fleeming Jenkin is a scientific engineer.

Now it seems to me that the difference between scientific and merely technical thought, not only in these but in all other instances which I have considered, is just this: Both of them make use of experience to direct human action; but while technical thought or skill enables a man to deal with the same circumstances that he has met with before, scientific thought enables him to deal with different circumstances that he has never met with before. But how can experience of one thing enable us to deal with another quite different thing? To answer this question we shall have to consider more closely the nature of scientific thought.

Let us take another example. You know that if you make a dot on a piece of paper, and then hold a piece of Iceland spar over it, you will see not one dot but two. A mineralogist, by measuring the angles of a crystal, can tell you whether or no it possesses this property without looking through it. He requires no scientific thought to do that. But Sir William Rowan Hamilton, the late Astronomer-Royal of Ireland, knowing these facts and also the explanation of them which Fresnel had given, thought about the subject, and he predicted that by looking through certain crystals in a particular direction we should see not two dots but a continuous circle. Mr. Lloyd made the experiment, and saw the circle, a result which had never been even suspected. This has always been considered one of the most signal instances of

[1] *On Braced Arches and Suspension Bridges.* Edinburgh: Neill, 1870.

scientific thought in the domain of physics. It is most distinctly an application of experience gained under certain circumstances to entirely different circumstances.

Now suppose that the night before coming down to Brighton you had dreamed of a railway accident caused by the engine getting frightened at a flock of sheep and jumping suddenly back over all the carriages; the result of which was that your head was unfortunately cut off, so that you had to put it in your hat-box and take it back home to be mended. There are, I fear, many persons even at this day, who would tell you that after such a dream it was unwise to travel by railway to Brighton. This is a proposal that you should take experience gained while you are asleep, when you have no common sense,—experience about a phantom railway, and apply it to guide you when you are awake and have common sense, in your dealings with a real railway. And yet this proposal is not dictated by scientific thought.

Now let us take the great example of Biology. I pass over the process of classification, which itself requires a great deal of scientific thought; in particular when a naturalist who has studied and monographed a fauna or a flora rather than a family is able at once to pick out the distinguishing characters required for the subdivision of an order quite new to him. Suppose that we possess all this minute and comprehensive knowledge of plants and animals and intermediate organisms, their affinities and differences, their structures and functions—a vast body of experience, collected by incalculable labour and devotion. Then comes Mr. Herbert Spencer: he takes that experience of life which is not human, which is apparently stationary, going on in exactly the same way from year to year, and he applies that to tell us how to deal with the changing characters of human nature and human society. How is it that experience of this sort, vast as it is, can guide us in a matter so different from itself? How does scientific thought, applied to the development of a kangaroo fœtus or the movement of the sap in exogens, make prediction possible for the first time in that most important of all sciences, the relations of man with man?

In the dark or unscientific ages men had another way of applying experience to altered circumstances. They believed, for example, that the plant called Jew's-ear, which does bear a certain resemblance to the human ear, was a useful cure for diseases of that organ. This doctrine of " signatures," as it was called, exercised an enormous influence on the medicine of the time. I need hardly tell you that it is hopelessly unscientific: yet it agrees with those other examples that we have been considering in this particular; that it applies experience about the shape of a plant—which is one circumstance connected with it—to dealings with its medicinal properties, which are other and different circumstances. Again, suppose that you had been frightened by a thunderstorm on land, or your heart had failed you in a storm at sea; if anyone then told you that in consequence of this you should always cultivate an unpleasant sensation in the pit of your stomach, till you took delight in it, that you should regulate your sane and sober life by the sensations of a moment of unreasoning terror: this advice would not be an example of scientific thought, yet it would be an application of past experience to new and different circumstances.

But you will already have observed what is the additional clause that we must add to our definition in order to describe scientific thought and that only. The step between experience about animals and dealings with changing humanity is the law of evolution. The step from errors in the calculated places of Uranus to the existence of Neptune is the law of gravitation. The step from the observed behaviour of crystals to conical refraction is made up of laws of light and geometry. The step from old bridges to new ones is the laws of elasticity and the strength of materials.

The step, then, from past experience to new circumstances must be made in accordance with an observed uniformity in the order of events. This uniformity has held good in the past in certain places; if it should also hold good in the future and in other places, then, being combined with our experience of the past, it enables us to predict the future, and to know what is going on elsewhere; so that we are able to regulate our conduct in accordance with this knowledge.

The aim of scientific thought, then, is to apply past experience to new circumstances; the instrument is an observed uniformity in the course of events. By the use of this instrument it gives us information transcending our experience, it enables us to infer things that we have not seen from things that we have seen; and the evidence for the truth of that information depends on our supposing that the uniformity holds good beyond our experience. I now want to consider this uniformity a little more closely; to show how the character of scientific thought and the force of its inferences depend upon the character of the uniformity of Nature. I cannot of course tell you all that is known of this character without writing an encyclopædia; but I shall confine myself to two points of it about which it seems to me that just now there is something to be said. I want to find out what we mean when we say that the uniformity of Nature is *exact*; and what we mean when we say that it is *reasonable*.

When a student is first introduced to those sciences which have come under the dominion of mathematics, a new and wonderful aspect of Nature bursts upon his view. He has been accustomed to regard things as essentially more or less vague. All the facts that he has hitherto known have been expressed qualitatively, with a little allowance for error on either side. Things which are let go fall to the ground. A very observant man may know also that they fall faster as they go along. But our student is shown that, after falling for one second in a vacuum, a body is going at the rate of thirty-two feet per second, that after falling for two seconds it is going twice as fast; after going two and a half seconds two and a half times as fast. If he makes the experiment, and finds a single inch per second too much or too little in the rate, one of two things must have happened:

either the law of falling bodies has been wrongly stated, or the experiment is not accurate—there is some mistake. He finds reason to think that the latter is always the case; the more carefully he goes to work, the more of the error turns out to belong to the experiment. Again, he may know that water consists of two gases, oxygen and hydrogen, combined; but he now learns that two pints of steam at a temperature of 150° centigrade will always make two pints of hydrogen and one pint of oxygen at the same temperature, all of them being pressed as much as the atmosphere is pressed. If he makes the experiment and gets rather more or less than a pint of oxygen, is the law disproved? No; the steam was impure, or there was some mistake. Myriads of analyses attest the law of combining volumes; the more carefully they are made, the more nearly they coincide with it. The aspects of the faces of a crystal are connected together by a geometrical law, by which, four of them being given, the rest can be found. The place of a planet at a given time is calculated by the law of gravitation; if it is half a second wrong, the fault is in the instrument, the observer, the clock, or the law; now, the more observations are made, the more of this fault is brought home to the instrument, the observer, and the clock. It is no wonder, then, that our student, contemplating these and many like instances, should be led to say: "I have been short-sighted; but I have now put on the spectacles of science which Nature had prepared for my eyes; I see that things have definite outlines, that the world is ruled by exact and rigid mathematical laws; καὶ, σύ, θεός, γεωμετρεῖς." It is our business to consider whether he is right in so concluding. Is the uniformity of Nature absolutely exact, or only more exact than our experiments?

At this point we have to make a very important distinction. There are two ways in which a law may be inaccurate. The first way is exemplified by that law of Galileo which I mentioned just now: that a body falling *in vacuo* acquires equal increase in velocity in equal times. No matter how many feet per second it is going, after an interval of a second it will be going thirty-two *more* feet per second. We now know that this rate of increase is not exactly the same at different heights, that it depends upon the distance of the body from the centre of the earth; so that the law is only approximate; instead of the increase of velocity being exactly *equal* in equal times, it itself increases very slowly as the body falls. We know also that this variation of the law from the truth is *too small to be perceived* by direct observation on the change of velocity. But suppose we have invented means for observing this, and have verified that the increase of velocity is inversely as the squared distance from the earth's centre. Still the law is not accurate; for the earth does not attract accurately towards her centre, and the direction of attraction is continually varying with the motion of the sea; the body will not even fall in a straight line. The sun and the planets, too, especially the moon, will produce deviations; yet the sum of all these errors will escape our new process of observation by being a great deal smaller than the necessary errors of that observation. But when these again have been allowed for, there is still the influence of the stars. In this case, however, we only give up one exact law for another. It may still be held that if the effect of every particle of matter in the universe on the falling body were calculated according to the law of gravitation, the body would move exactly as this calculation required. And if it were objected that the body must be slightly magnetic or diamagnetic, while there are magnets not an infinite way off; that a very minute repulsion, even at sensible distances, accompanies the attraction; it might be replied that these phenomena are themselves subject to exact laws, and that when *all* the laws have been taken into account, the actual motion will exactly correspond with the calculated motion.

I suppose there is hardly a physical student (unless he has specially considered the matter) who would not at once assent to the statement I have just made; that if we knew all about it, Nature would be found universally subject to exact numerical laws. But let us just consider for another moment what this means.

The word "exact" has a practical and a theoretical meaning. When a grocer weighs you out a certain quantity of sugar very carefully and says it is exactly a pound, he means that the difference between the mass of the sugar and that of the pound weight he employs is too small to be detected by his scales. If a chemist had made a special investigation, wishing to be as accurate as he could, and told you this was exactly a pound of sugar, he would mean that the mass of the sugar differed from that of a certain standard piece of platinum by a quantity too small to be detected by *his* means of weighing, which are a thousandfold more accurate than the grocer's. But what would a mathematician mean, if he made the same statement? He would mean this. Suppose the mass of the standard pound to be represented by a length, say a foot, measured on a certain line; so that half a pound would be represented by six inches, and so on. And let the difference between the mass of the sugar and that of the standard pound be drawn upon the same line to the same scale. Then, if that difference were magnified an infinite number of times, it would still be invisible. This is the theoretical meaning of exactness; the practical meaning is only very close approximation; *how* close, depends upon the circumstances. The knowledge then of an exact law in the theoretical sense would be equivalent to an infinite observation. I do not say that such knowledge is impossible to man; but I do say that it would be absolutely different in kind from any knowledge that we possess at present.

I shall be told, no doubt, that we do possess a great deal of knowledge of this kind, in the form of geometry and mechanics; and that it is just the example of these sciences that has led men to look for exactness in other quarters. If this had been said to me in the last century, I should not have known what to reply. But it happens that about the beginning of the present century the foundations of geometry were criticised independently by two mathematicians, Lobatschewsky [1] and the im-

---

[1] *Geometrische Untersuchungen zur Theorie der Parallellinien.* Berlin, 1840. Translated by Hoüel. Gauthier-Villars, 1866.

mortal Gauss; [1] whose results have been extended and generalised more recently by Riemann [2] and Helmholtz. [3] And the conclusion to which these investigations lead is that, although the assumptions which were very properly made by the ancient geometers are practically exact— that is to say, more exact than experiment can be—for such finite things as we have to deal with, and such portions of space as we can reach; yet the truth of them for very much larger things, or very much smaller things, or parts of space which are at present beyond our reach, is a matter to be decided by experiment, when its powers are considerably increased. I want to make as clear as possible the real state of this question at present, because it is often supposed to be a question of words or metaphysics, whereas it is a very distinct and simple question of fact. I am supposed to know then that the three angles of a rectilinear triangle are exactly equal to two right angles. Now suppose that three points are taken in space, distant from one another as far as the Sun is from α Centauri, and that the shortest distances between these points are drawn so as to form a triangle. And suppose the angles of this triangle to be very accurately measured and added together; this can at present be done so accurately that the error shall certainly be less than one minute, less therefore than the five-thousandth part of a right angle. Then I do not know that this sum would differ at all from two right angles; but also I do not know that the difference would be less than ten degrees, or the ninth part of a right angle. [4] And I have reasons for not knowing.

This example is exceedingly important as showing the connection between exactness and universality. It is

[1] Letter to Schumacher, Nov. 28, 1846 (refers to 1792).

[2] *Ueber die Hypothesen welche der Geometrie zu Grunde liegen.* Göttingen, Abhandl., 1866–67. Translated by Hoüel in *Annali di Matematica*, Milan, vol. iii.

[3] *The Axioms of Geometry*, Academy, vol. i. p. 128 (a popular exposition). [And see now his article in *Mind*, No. III.]

[4] Assuming that parallax observations prove the deviation less than half a second for a triangle whose vertex is at the star and base a diameter of the earth's orbit.

found that the deviation if it exists must be nearly proportional to the area of the triangle. So that the error in the case of a triangle whose sides are a mile long would be obtained by dividing that in the case I have just been considering by four hundred quadrillions; the result must be a quantity inconceivably small which no experiment could detect. But, between this inconceivably small error and no error at all, there is fixed an enormous gulf; the gulf between practical and theoretical exactness, and, what is even more important, the gulf between what is practically universal and what is theoretically universal. I say that a law is practically universal which is more exact than experiment for all cases that might be got at by such experiments as we can make. We assume this kind of universality, and we find that it pays us to assume it. But a law would be theoretically universal if it were true of all cases whatever; and this is what we do not know of any law at all.

I said there were two ways in which a law might be inexact. There is a law of gases which asserts that when you compress a perfect gas the pressure of the gas increases exactly in the proportion in which the volume diminishes. Exactly; that is to say, the law is more accurate than the experiment, and experiments are corrected by means of the law. But it so happens that this law has been explained; we know precisely what it is that happens when a gas is compressed. We know that a gas consists of a vast number of separate molecules, rushing about in all directions with all manner of velocities, but so that the mean velocity of the molecules of air in this room, for example, is about twenty miles a minute. The pressure of the gas on any surface with which it is in contact is nothing more than the impact of these small particles upon it. On any surface large enough to be seen there are millions of these impacts in a second. If the space in which the gas is confined be diminished, the average rate at which the impacts take place will be increased in the same proportion; and because of the enormous number of them, the actual rate is always exceedingly close to the average. But the law is one of statistics; its accuracy depends on the enormous numbers involved; and so, from the nature of the case, its exactness cannot be theoretical or absolute.

Nearly all the laws of gases have received these statistical explanations; electric and magnetic attraction and repulsion have been treated in a similar manner; and an hypothesis of this sort has been suggested even for the law of gravity. On the other hand the manner in which the molecules of a gas interfere with each other proves that they repel one another inversely as the fifth power of the distance; [1] so that we here find at the basis of a statistical explanation a law which has the form of theoretical exactness.   Which of these forms is to win? It seems to me again that we do not know, and that the recognition of our ignorance is the surest way to get rid of it.

The world in general has made just the remark that I have attributed to a fresh student of the applied sciences. As the discoveries of Galileo, Kepler, Newton, Dalton, Cavendish, Gauss, displayed ever new phenomena following mathematical laws, the theoretical exactness of the physical universe was taken for granted.   Now, when people are hopelessly ignorant of a thing, they quarrel about the source of their knowledge.   Accordingly, many maintained that we know these exact laws by intuition. These said always one true thing, that we did not know them from experience.   Others said that they were really given in the facts, and adopted ingenious ways of hiding the gulf between the two.   Others again deduced from transcendental considerations sometimes the laws themselves, and sometimes what through imperfect information they supposed to be the laws.   But more serious consequences arose when these conceptions derived from Physics were carried over into the field of Biology.   Sharp lines of division were made between kingdoms and classes and orders; an animal was described as a miracle to the vegetable world; specific differences which are practically permanent within the range of history were regarded as permanent through all time; a sharp line was drawn

[1] [This statement of the law has since been abandoned.]

between organic and inorganic matter. Further investigation, however, has shown that accuracy had been prematurely attributed to the science, and has filled up all the gulfs and gaps that hasty observers had invented. The animal and vegetable kingdoms have a debatable ground between them, occupied by beings that have the characters of both and yet belong distinctly to neither. Classes and orders shade into one another all along their common boundary. Specific differences turn out to be the work of time. The line dividing organic matter from inorganic, if drawn to-day, must be moved to-morrow to another place; and the chemist will tell you that the distinction has now no place in his science except in a technical sense for the convenience of studying carbon compounds by themselves. In Geology the same tendency gave birth to the doctrine of distinct periods, marked out by the character of the strata deposited in them all over the sea; a doctrine than which, perhaps, no ancient cosmogony has been further from the truth, or done more harm to the progress of science. Refuted many years ago by Mr. Herbert Spencer,[1] it has now fairly yielded to an attack from all sides at once, and may be left in peace.

When then we say that the uniformity which we observe in the course of events is exact and universal, we mean no more than this: that we are able to state general rules which are far more exact than direct experiment, and which apply to all cases that we are at present likely to come across. It is important to notice, however, the effect of such exactness as we observe upon the nature of inference. When a telegram arrived stating that Dr. Livingstone had been found by Mr. Stanley, what was the process by which you inferred the finding of Dr. Livingstone from the appearance of the telegram? You assumed over and over again the existence of uniformity in nature. That the newspapers had behaved as they generally do in regard to telegraphic messages; that the clerks had followed the known laws of the action of

[1] "Illogical Geology," in *Essays*, vol. i. Originally published in 1859.

clerks; that electricity had behaved in the cable exactly as it behaves in the laboratory; that the actions of Mr. Stanley were related to his motives by the same uniformities that affect the actions of other men; that Dr. Livingstone's handwriting conformed to the curious rule by which an ordinary man's handwriting may be recognised as having persistent characteristics even at different periods of his life. But you had a right to be much more sure about some of these inferences than about others. The law of electricity was known with practical exactness, and the conclusions derived from it were the surest things of all. The law about the handwriting, belonging to a portion of physiology which is unconnected with consciousness, was known with less, but still with considerable accuracy. But the laws of human action in which consciousness is concerned are still so far from being completely analysed and reduced to an exact form that the inferences which you made by their help were felt to have only a provisional force. It is possible that by and by, when psychology has made enormous advances and become an exact science, we may be able to give to testimony the sort of weight which we give to the inferences of physical science. It will then be possible to conceive a case which will show how completely the whole process of inference depends on our assumption of uniformity. Suppose that testimony, having reached the ideal force I have imagined, were to assert that a certain river runs uphill. You could infer nothing at all. The arm of inference would be paralysed, and the sword of truth broken in its grasp; and reason could only sit down and wait until recovery restored her limb, and further experience gave her new weapons.

I want in the next place to consider what we mean when we say that the uniformity which we have observed in the course of events is *reasonable* as well as exact.

No doubt the first form of this idea was suggested by the marvellous adaptation of certain natural structures to special functions. The first impression of those who studied comparative anatomy was that every part of the animal frame was fitted with extraordinary completeness for the work that it had to do. I say extraordinary, because at the time the most familiar examples of this adaptation were manufactures produced by human ingenuity; and the completeness and minuteness of natural adaptations were seen to be far in advance of these. The mechanism of limbs and joints was seen to be adapted, far better than any existing ironwork, to those motions and combinations of motion which were most useful to the particular organisms. The beautiful and complicated apparatus of sensation caught up indications from the surrounding medium, sorted them, analysed them, and transmitted the results to the brain in a manner with which, at the time I am speaking of, no artificial contrivance could compete. Hence the belief grew amongst physiologists that every structure which they found must have its function and subserve some useful purpose; a belief which was not without its foundation in fact, and which certainly (as Dr. Whewell remarks) has done admirable service in promoting the growth of physiology. Like all beliefs found successful in one subject, it was carried over into another, of which a notable example is given in the speculations of Count Rumford about the physical properties of water. Pure water attains its greatest density at a temperature of about $39\frac{1}{2}°$ Fahrenheit; it expands and becomes lighter whether it is cooled or heated, so as to alter that temperature. Hence it was concluded that water in this state must be at the bottom of the sea, and that by such means the sea was kept from freezing all through; as it was supposed must happen if the greatest density had been that of ice. Here then was a substance whose properties were eminently adapted to secure an end essential to the maintenance of life upon the earth. In short, men came to the conclusion that the order of nature was reasonable in the sense that everything was adapted to some good end.

Further consideration, however, has led men out of that conclusion in two different ways. First, it was seen that the facts of the case had been wrongly stated. Cases were found of wonderfully complicated structures that served no purpose at all; like the teeth of that whale of which you heard in Section D the other day, or of the Dugong, which has a horny palate covering them all up and used instead of them; like the eyes of the unborn mole, that are never used, though perfect as those of a mouse until the skull opening closes up, cutting them off from the brain, when they dry up and become incapable of use; like the outsides of your own ears, which are absolutely of no use to you. And when human contrivances were more advanced it became clear that the natural adaptations were subject to criticism. The eye, regarded as an optical instrument of human manufacture, was thus described by Helmholtz—the physiologist who learned physics for the sake of his physiology, and mathematics for the sake of his physics, and is now in the first rank of all three. He said, " If an optician sent me that as an instrument, I should send it back to him with grave reproaches for the carelessness of his work, and demand the return of my money."

The extensions of the doctrine into Physics were found to be still more at fault. That remarkable property of pure water, which was to have kept the sea from freezing, does not belong to salt water, of which the sea itself is composed. It was found, in fact, that the idea of a reasonable adaptation of means to ends, useful as it had been in its proper sphere, could yet not be called universal, or applied to the order of nature as a whole.

Secondly, this idea has given way because it has been superseded by a higher and more general idea of what is reasonable, which has the advantage of being applicable to a large portion of physical phenomena besides. Both the adaptation and the non-adaptation which occur in organic structures have been *explained*. The scientific thought of Dr. Darwin, of Mr. Herbert Spencer, and of Mr. Wallace, has described that hitherto unknown process of adaptation as consisting of perfectly well-known and familiar processes. There are two kinds of these: the direct processes, in which the physical changes required to produce a structure are worked out by the very actions for which that structure becomes adapted—as the

backbone or notochord has been modified from generation to generation by the bendings which it has under-
gone; and the indirect processes included under the
head of Natural Selection—the reproduction of children
slightly different from their parents, and the survival of
those which are best fitted to hold their own in the
struggle for existence. Naturalists might give you some
idea of the rate at which we are getting explanations of
the evolution of all parts of animals and plants—the
growth of the skeleton, of the nervous system and its
mind, of leaf and flower. But what then do we mean by
explanation?

We were considering just now an explanation of a law
of gases—the law according to which pressure increases
in the same proportion in which volume diminishes.
The explanation consisted in supposing that a gas is
made up of a vast number of minute particles always
flying about and striking against one another, and then
showing that the rate of impact of such a crowd of
particles on the sides of the vessel containing them would
vary exactly as the pressure is found to vary. Suppose
the vessel to have parallel sides, and that there is only one
particle rushing backwards and forwards between them;
then it is clear that if we bring the sides together to half
the distance, the particle will hit each of them twice as
often, or the pressure will be doubled. Now it turns
out that this would be just as true for millions of particles
as for one, and when they are flying in all directions
instead of only in one direction and its opposite. Observe now; it is a perfectly well-known and familiar thing
that a body should strike against an opposing surface
and bound off again; and it is a mere everyday occur-
rence that what has only half so far to go should be back
in half the time; but that pressure should be strictly
proportional to density is a comparatively strange, unfamiliar phenomenon. The explanation describes the
unknown and unfamiliar as being made up of the known
and the familiar; and this, it seems to me, is the true
meaning of explanation.[1]

[1] This view differs from those of Mr. J. S. Mill and Mr. Herbert

Here is another instance. If small pieces of camphor are dropped into water, they will begin to spin round and swim about in a most marvellous way. Mr. Tomlinson gave, I believe, the explanation of this. We must observe, to begin with, that every liquid has a skin which holds it; you can see that to be true in the case of a drop, which looks as if it were held in a bag. But the tension of this skin is greater in some liquids than in others; and it is greater in camphor and water than in pure water. When the camphor is dropped into water it begins to dissolve and get surrounded with camphor and water instead of water. If the fragment of camphor were exactly symmetrical, nothing more would happen; the tension would be greater in its immediate neighbourhood, but no motion would follow. The camphor, however, is irregular in shape; it dissolves more on one side than the other: and consequently gets pulled about, because the tension of the skin is greater where the camphor is most dissolved. Now it is probable that this is not nearly so satisfactory an explanation to you as it was to me when I was first told of it; and for this reason. By that time I was already perfectly familiar with the notion of a skin upon the surface of liquids, and I had been taught by means of it to work out problems in capillarity. The explanation was therefore a description of the unknown phenomenon which I did not know how to deal with as made up of known phenomena which I did know how to deal with. But to many of you possibly the liquid skin may seem quite as strange and unaccountable as the motion of camphor on water.

And this brings me to consider the source of the pleasure we derive from an explanation. By known and familiar I mean that which we know how to deal with, either by action in the ordinary sense, or by active thought. When, therefore, that which we do not know how to deal with is described as made up of things that

---

Spencer in requiring every explanation to contain an addition to our knowledge about the thing explained. Both these writers regard subsumption under a general law as a species of explanation. See also Ferrier's *Remains*, vol. ii. p. 436.

we do know how to deal with, we have that sense of increased power which is the basis of all higher pleasures. Of course we may afterwards, by association, come to take pleasure in explanation for its own sake. Are we then to say that the observed order of events is reasonable, in the sense that all of it admits of explanation? That a process may be capable of explanation, it must break up into simpler constituents which are already familiar to us. Now, first, the process may itself be simple, and not break up; secondly, it may break up into elements which are as unfamiliar and impracticable as the original process.

It is an explanation of the moon's motion to say that she is a falling body, only she is going so fast and is so far off that she falls quite round to the other side of the earth, instead of hitting it; and so goes on for ever. But it is no explanation to say that a body falls because of gravitation. That means that the motion of the body may be resolved into a motion of every one of its particles towards every one of the particles of the earth, with an acceleration inversely as the square of the distance between them. But this attraction of two particles must always, I think, be less familiar than the original falling body, however early the children of the future begin to read their Newton. Can the attraction itself be explained? Le Sage said that there is an everlasting hail of innumerable small ether-particles from all sides, and that the two material particles shield each other from this and so get pushed together. This is an explanation; it may or may not be a true one. The attraction may be an ultimate simple fact; or it may be made up of simpler facts utterly unlike anything that we know at present; and in either of these cases there is no explanation. We have no right to conclude, then, that the order of events is always capable of being explained.

There is yet another way in which it is said that Nature is reasonable; namely, inasmuch as every effect has a cause. What do we mean by this?

In asking this question, we have entered upon an appalling task. The word represented by " cause " has sixty-four meanings in Plato and forty-eight in Aristotle. These were men who liked to know as near as might be what they meant; but how many meanings it has had in the writings of the myriads of people who have not tried to know what they meant by it will, I hope, never be counted. It would not only be the height of presumption in me to attempt to fix the meaning of a word which has been used by so grave authority in so many and various senses; but it would seem a thankless task to do that once more which has been done so often at sundry times and in divers manners before. And yet without this we cannot determine what we mean by saying that the order of nature is reasonable. I shall evade the difficulty by telling you Mr. Grote's opinion.[1] You come to a scarecrow and ask, What is the cause of this? You find that a man made it to frighten the birds. You go away and say to yourself: "Everything resembles this scarecrow. Everything has a purpose." And from that day the word " cause " means for you what Aristotle meant by " final cause." Or you go into a hairdresser's shop, and wonder what turns the wheel to which the rotatory brush is attached. On investigating other parts of the premises, you find a man working away at a handle. Then you go away and say: " Everything is like that wheel. If I investigated enough, I should always find a man at a handle." And the man at the handle, or whatever corresponds to him, is from henceforth known to you as " cause."

And so generally. When you have made out any sequence of events to your entire satisfaction, so that you know all about it, the laws involved being so familiar that you seem to see how the beginning must have been followed by the end, then you apply that as a simile to all other events whatever, and your idea of cause is determined by it. Only when a case arises, as it always must, to which the simile will not apply, you do not confess to yourself that it was only a simile and need not apply to everything, but you say: " The cause of that event is a mystery which must remain for ever unknown to me."

[1] Plato, vol. ii (*Phædo*).

On equally just grounds the nervous system of my umbrella is a mystery which must remain for ever unknown to me. My umbrella has no nervous system; and the event to which your simile did not apply has no cause in your sense of the word. When we say then that every effect has a cause, we mean that every event is connected with something in a way that might make somebody call that the cause of it. But I, at least, have never yet seen any single meaning of the word that could be fairly applied to the *whole* order of nature.

From this remark I cannot even except an attempt recently made by Mr. Bain to give the word a universal meaning, though I desire to speak of that attempt with the greatest respect. Mr. Bain [1] wishes to make the word " cause " hang on in some way to what we call the law of energy; but though I speak with great diffidence I do think a careful consideration will show that the introduction of this word " cause " can only bring confusion into a matter which is distinct and clear enough to those who have taken the trouble to understand what energy means. It would be impossible to explain that this evening; but I may mention that " energy " is a technical term out of mathematical physics, which requires of most men a good deal of careful study to understand it accurately.

Let us pass on to consider, with all the reverence which it demands, another opinion held by great numbers of the philosophers who have lived in the Brightening Ages of Europe; the opinion that at the basis of the natural order there is something which we can know to be *unreasonable*, to evade the processes of human thought. The opinion is set forth first by Kant, so far as I know, in the form of his famous doctrine of the antinomies or contradictions, a later form [2] of which I will endeavour to explain to you. It is said, then, that space must

---

[1] *Inductive Logic*, chap, iv. ,

[2] That of Mr. Herbert Spencer, *First Principles*. I believe Kant himself would have admitted that the antinomies do not exist for the empiricist. [Much less does he say that either of a pair of antinomies must be true. The real Kantian position is that both assertions are illegitimate.]

either be infinite or have a boundary. Now you cannot conceive infinite space; and you cannot conceive that there should be any end to it. Here, then, are two things, one of which must be true, while each of them is inconceivable; so that our thoughts about space are hedged in as it were, by a contradiction. Again, it is said that matter must either be infinitely divisible, or must consist of small particles incapable of further division. Now you cannot conceive a piece of matter divided into an infinite number of parts, while, on the other hand, you cannot conceive a piece of matter, however small, which absolutely cannot be divided into two pieces; for, however great the forces are which join the parts of it together, you can imagine stronger forces able to tear it in pieces. Here, again, there are two statements, one of which must be true, while each of them is separately inconceivable; so that our thoughts about matter also are hedged in by a contradiction. There are several other cases of the same thing, but I have selected these two as instructive examples. And the conclusion to which philosophers were led by the contemplation of them was that on every side, when we approach the limits of existence a contradiction must stare us in the face. The doctrine has been developed and extended by the great successors of Kant; and this unreasonable, or unknowable, which is also called the absolute and the unconditioned, has been set forth in various ways as that which we know to be the true basis of all things. As I said before, I approach this doctrine with all the reverence which should be felt for that which has guided the thoughts of so many of the wisest of mankind. Nevertheless, I shall endeavour to show that in these cases of supposed contradiction there is always something which we do not know now, but of which we cannot be sure that we shall be ignorant next year. The doctrine is an attempt to found a positive statement upon this ignorance, which can hardly be regarded as justifiable. Spinoza said, " A free man thinks of nothing so little as of death; " it seems to me we may parallel this maxim in the case of thought, and say, " A wise man only remembers his ignorance in order to destroy it." A boundary is that which divides two adjacent portions of space. The question, then, " Has space (in general) a boundary? " involves a contradiction in terms, and is, therefore, unmeaning. But the question, " Does space contain a finite number of cubic miles, or an infinite number? " is a perfectly intelligible and reasonable question which remains to be answered by experiment.[1] The surface of the sea would still contain a finite number of square miles, if there were no land to bound it. Whether or no the space in which we live is of this nature remains to be seen. If its extent is finite, we may quite possibly be able to assign that extent next year; if, on the other hand, it has no end, it is true that the knowledge of that fact would be quite different from any knowledge we at present possess, but we have no right to say that such knowledge is impossible. Either the question will be settled once for all, or the extent of space will be shown to be greater than a quantity which will increase from year to year with the improvement of our sources of knowledge. Either alternative is perfectly conceivable, and there is no contradiction. Observe especially that the supposed contradiction arises from the assumption of theoretical exactness in the laws of geometry. The other case that I mentioned has a very similar origin. The idea of a piece of matter the parts of which are held together by forces, and are capable of being torn asunder by greater forces, is entirely derived from the large pieces of matter which we have to deal with. We do not know whether this idea applies in any sense even to the *molecules* of gases; still less can we apply it to the *atoms* of which they are composed. The word " force " is used of two phenomena: the pressure, which when two bodies are in contact connects the motion of each with the position of the other; and attraction or repulsion,—that is to say, a change of velocity in one body depending on the position of some other body which is not in contact with it. We do not know that

---

[1] The very important distinction between *unboundedness* and *infinite extent* is made by Riemann, *loc. cit.*

there is anything corresponding to either of these phenomena in the case of a molecule. A meaning can, however, be given to the question of the divisibility of matter in this way. We may ask if there is any piece of matter so small that its properties as matter depend upon its remaining all in one piece. This question is reasonable; but we cannot answer it at present, though we are not at all sure that we shall be equally ignorant next year. If there is no such piece of matter, no such limit to the division which shall leave it matter, the knowledge of that fact would be different from any of our present knowledge; but we have no right to say that it is impossible. If, on the other hand, there *is* a limit, it is quite possible that we may have measured it by the time the Association meets at Bradford. Again, when we are told that the infinite extent of space, for example, is something that we cannot conceive at present, we may reply that this is only natural, since our experience has never yet supplied us with the means of conceiving such things. But then we cannot be sure that the facts will not make us learn to conceive them; in which case they will cease to be inconceivable. In fact, the putting of limits to human conception must always involve the assumption that our previous experience is universally valid in a theoretical sense; an assumption which we have already seen reason to reject. Now you will see that our consideration of this opinion has led us to the true sense of the assertion that the Order of Nature is reasonable. If you will allow me to define a reasonable question as one which is asked in terms of ideas justified by previous experience, without itself contradicting that experience, then we may say, as the result of our investigation, that to every reasonable question there is an intelligible answer which either we or posterity may know.

We have, then, come somehow to the following conclusions. By scientific thought we mean the application of past experience to new circumstances by means of an observed order of events. By saying that this order of events is exact we mean that it is exact enough to correct experiments by, but we do not mean that it is theoretically or absolutely exact, because we do not know. The process of inference we found to be in itself an assumption of uniformity, and we found that, as the known exactness of the uniformity became greater, the stringency of the inference increased. By saying that the order of events is reasonable we do not mean that everything has a purpose, or that everything can be explained, or that everything has a cause; for neither of these is true. But we mean that to every reasonable question there is an intelligible answer, which either we or posterity may know *by the exercise of scientific thought.*

For I specially wish you not to go away with the idea that the exercise of scientific thought is properly confined to the subjects from which my illustrations have been chiefly drawn to-night. When the Roman jurists applied their experience of Roman citizens to dealings between citizens and aliens, showing by the difference of their actions that they regarded the circumstances as essentially different, they laid the foundations of that great structure which has guided the social progress of Europe. That procedure was an instance of strictly scientific thought. When a poet finds that he has to move a strange new world which his predecessors have not moved; when, nevertheless, he catches fire from their flashes, arms from their armoury, sustentation from their footprints, the procedure by which he applies old experience to new circumstances is nothing greater or less than scientific thought. When the moralist, studying the conditions of society and the ideas of right and wrong which have come down to us from a time when war was the normal condition of man and success in war the only chance of survival, evolves from them the conditions and ideas which must accompany a time of peace, when the comradeship of equals is the condition of national success; the process by which he does this is scientific thought and nothing else. Remember, then, that it is the guide of action; that the truth which it arrives at is not that which we can ideally contemplate without error, but that which we may act upon without fear; and you cannot fail to see that scientific thought is not an accompaniment or condition of human progress, but human progress itself.   And for this reason the question what its characters are, of which I have so inadequately endeavoured to give you some glimpse, is the question of all questions for the human race.

RIGHT AND WRONG: THE SCIENTIFIC
GROUND OF THEIR DISTINCTION [1]

THE questions which are here to be considered are
especially and peculiarly everybody's questions. It is
not everybody's business to be an engineer, or a doctor,
or a carpenter, or a soldier; but it is everybody's business
to be a citizen. The doctrines and precepts which guide
the practice of the good engineer are of interest to him
who uses them and to those whose business it is to investigate them by mechanical science; the rest of us
neither obey nor disobey them. But the doctrines and
precepts of morality, which guide the practice of the
good citizen, are of interest to all; they must be either
obeyed or disobeyed by every human being who is not
hopelessly and for ever separated from the rest of mankind. No one can say, therefore, that in this inquiry
we are not minding our own business, that we are
meddling with other men's affairs. We are in fact
studying the principles of our profession, so far as we are
able; a necessary thing for every man who wishes to do
good work in it.

Along with the character of universal interest which
belongs to our subject there goes another. What is
everybody's practical business is also to a large extent
what everybody knows; and it may be reasonably expected that a discourse about Right and Wrong will be
full of platitudes and truisms. The expectation is a
just one. The considerations I have to offer are of the
very oldest and the very simplest commonplace and
common sense; and no one can be more astonished than
I am that there should be any reason to speak of them at
all. But there is reason to speak of them, because
platitudes are not all of one kind. Some platitudes have
a definite meaning and a practical application, and are
established by the uniform and long-continued experience
of all people. Other platitudes, having no definite
meaning and no practical application, seem not to be

[1] Sunday Lecture Society, November 7, 1875; *Fortnightly
Review*, December, 1875.

worth anybody's while to test; and these are quite
sufficiently established by mere assertion, if it is audacious
enough to begin with and persistent enough afterwards.
It is in order to distinguish these two kinds of platitude
from one another, and to make sure that those which we
retain form a body of doctrine consistent with itself and
with the rest of our beliefs, that we undertake this
examination of obvious and widespread principles.

First of all, then, what are the facts?

We say that it is wrong to murder, to steal, to tell lies,
and that it is right to take care of our families. When
we say in this sense that one action is right and another
wrong, we have a certain feeling towards the action
which is peculiar and not quite like any other feeling.
It is clearly a feeling towards the action and not towards
the man who does it; because we speak of hating the
sin and loving the sinner. We might reasonably dislike
a man whom we knew or suspected to be a murderer,
because of the natural fear that he might murder us;
and we might like our own parents for taking care of us.
But everybody knows that these feelings are something
quite different from the feeling which condemns murder
as a wrong thing, and approves parental care as a right
thing. I say nothing here about the possibility of
analysing this feeling, or proving that it arises by combination of other feelings; all I want to notice is that it
is as distinct and recognisable as the feeling of pleasure
in a sweet taste or of displeasure at a toothache. In
speaking of right and wrong, we speak of qualities of
action which arouse definite feelings that everybody
knows and recognises. It is not necessary, then, to give
a definition at the outset; we are going to use familiar
terms which have a definite meaning in the same sense
in which everybody uses them. We may ultimately
come to something like a definition; but what we have to
do first is to collect the facts and see what can be made of
them, just as if we were going to talk about limestone,
or parents and children, or fuel.[1]

It is easy to conceive that murder and theft and neglect

[1] These subjects have been treated in other lectures.

of the young might be considered wrong in a very simple state of society. But we find at present that the condemnation of these actions does not stand alone; it goes with the condemnation of a great number of other actions which seem to be included with the obviously criminal action in a sort of general rule. The wrongness of murder, for example, belongs in a less degree to any form of bodily injury that one man may inflict on another; and it is even extended so as to include injuries to his reputation or his feelings. I make these more refined precepts follow in the train of the more obvious and rough ones, because this appears to have been the traditional order of their establishment. "He that makes his neighbour blush in public," says the Mishna, "is as if he had shed his blood." In the same way the rough condemnation of stealing carries with it a condemnation of more refined forms of dishonesty; we do not hesitate to say that it is wrong for a tradesman to adulterate his goods, or for a labourer to scamp his work. We not only say that it is wrong to tell lies, but that it is wrong to deceive in other more ingenious ways; wrong to use words so that they shall have one sense to some people and another sense to other people; wrong to suppress the truth when that suppression leads to false belief in others. And again, the duty of parents towards their children is seen to be a special case of a very large and varied class of duties towards that great family to which we belong—to the fatherland and them that dwell therein. The word *duty*, which I have here used, has as definite a sense to the general mind as the words *right* and *wrong*; we say that it is right to do our duty, and wrong to neglect it. These duties to the community serve in our minds to explain and define our duties to individuals. It is wrong to kill anyone; unless we are an executioner, when it may be our duty to kill a criminal; or a soldier, when it may be our duty to kill the enemy of our country; and in general it is wrong to injure any man in any way in our private capacity and for our own sakes. Thus if a man injures us, it is only right to retaliate on behalf of other men. Of two men on a desert island, if one takes away the other's cloak, it may or may not be right for the other to let him have his coat also; but if a man takes away my cloak while we both live in society, it is my duty to use such means as I can to prevent him from taking away other people's cloaks. Observe that I am endeavouring to describe the facts of the moral feelings of Englishmen, such as they are now.

The last remark leads us to another platitude of exceedingly ancient date. We said that it was wrong to injure any man in our private capacity and for our own sakes. A rule like this differs from all the others that we have considered, because it not only deals with physical acts, words and deeds which can be observed and known by others, but also with thoughts which are known only to the man himself. Who can tell whether a given act of punishment was done from a private or from a public motive? Only the agent himself. And yet if the punishment was just and within the law, we should condemn the man in the one case and approve him in the other. This pursuit of the actions of men to their very sources, in the feelings which they only can know, is as ancient as any morality we know of, and extends to the whole range of it. Injury to another man arises from anger, malice, hatred, revenge; these feelings are condemned as wrong. But feelings are not immediately under our control, in the same way that overt actions are: I can shake anybody by the hand if I like, but I cannot always feel friendly to him. Nevertheless we can pay attention to such aspects of the circumstances, and we can put ourselves into such conditions, that our feelings get gradually modified in one way or the other; we form a habit of checking our anger by calling up certain images and considerations, whereby in time the offending passion is brought into subjection and control. Accordingly we say that it is right to acquire and to exercise this control; and the control is supposed to exist whenever we say that one feeling or disposition of mind is right and another wrong. Thus, in connection with the precept against stealing, we condemn envy and covetousness; we applaud a sensitive honesty which shudders at anything

underhand or dishonourable.   In connection with the
rough precept against lying, we have built up and are still
building a great fabric of intellectual morality, whereby
a man is forbidden to tell lies to himself, and is com-
manded to practise candour and fairness and open-
mindedness in his judgments, and to labour zealously in
pursuit of the truth.   And in connection with the duty to
our families, we say that it is right to cultivate public
spirit, a quick sense of sympathy, and all that belongs to a
social disposition.

Two other words are used in this connection which it
seems necessary to mention.   When we regard an action
as right or wrong for ourselves, this feeling about the
action impels us to do it or not to do it, as the case may
be.   We may say that the moral sense acts in this case
as a motive; meaning by moral sense only the feeling in
regard to an action which is considered as right or wrong,
and by motive something which impels us to act.   Of
course there may be other motives at work at the same
time, and it does not at all follow that we shall do the
right action or abstain from the wrong one.   This we all
know to our cost.   But still our feeling about the rightness or wrongness of an action does operate as a motive
when we think of the action as being done by us; and
when so operating it is called *conscience*.   I have nothing
to do at present with the questions about conscience,
whether it is a result of education, whether it can be
explained by self-love, and so forth; I am only concerned
in describing well-known facts, and in getting as clear as
I can about the meaning of well-known words.   Conscience, then, is the whole aggregate of our feelings about
actions as being right or wrong, regarded as tending to
make us do the right actions and avoid the wrong ones.
We also say sometimes, in answer to the question,
"How do you know that this is right or wrong?"
"My conscience tells me so."   And this way of speaking
is quite analogous to other expressions of the same form;
thus if I put my hand into water, and you ask me how I
know that it is hot, I might say, "My feeling of warmth
tells me so."

When we consider a right or a wrong action as done by another person, we think of that person as worthy of moral approbation or reprobation. He may be punished or not; but in any case this feeling towards him is quite different from the feeling of dislike towards a person injurious to us, or of disappointment at a machine which will not go.

Whenever we can morally approve or disapprove a man for his action, we say that he is morally responsible for it, and *vice versa*. To say that a man is not morally responsible for his actions is the same thing as to say that it would be unreasonable to praise or blame him for them.

The statement that we ourselves are morally responsible is somewhat more complicated, but the meaning is very easily made out; namely, that another person may reasonably regard our actions as right or wrong, and may praise or blame us for them.

We can now, I suppose, understand one another pretty clearly in using the words " right " and " wrong," " conscience," " responsibility "; and we have made a rapid survey of the facts of the case in our own country at the present time. Of course I do not pretend that this survey in any way approaches to completeness; but it will supply us at least with enough facts to enable us to deal always with concrete examples instead of remaining in generalities; and it may serve to show pretty fairly what the moral sense of an Englishman is like. We must next consider what account we can give of these facts by the scientific method.

But first let us stop to note that we really have used the scientific method in making this first step; and also that to the same extent the method has been used by all serious moralists. Some would have us define virtue, to begin with, in terms of some other thing which is not virtue, and then work out from our definition all the details of what we ought to do. So Plato said that virtue was knowledge, Aristotle that it was the golden mean, and Bentham said that the right action was that which conduced to the greatest happiness of the greatest

number. But so also, in physical speculations, Thales
said that everything was Water, and Heraclitus said it
was All-becoming, and Empedocles said it was made out
of Four Elements, and Pythagoras said it was Number.
But we only began to know about things when people
looked straight at the facts, and made what they could
out of them; and that is the only way in which we can
know anything about right and wrong. Moreover, it
is the way in which the great moralists have set to work,
when they came to treat of verifiable things and not of
theories all in the air. A great many people think of a
prophet as a man who, all by himself, or from some secret
source, gets the belief that this thing is right and that
thing wrong. And then (they imagine) he gets up and
goes about persuading other people to feel as he does
about it; and so it becomes a part of their conscience,
and a new duty is created. This may be in some cases,
but I have never met with any example of it in history.
When Socrates puzzled the Greeks by asking them what
they precisely meant by Goodness and Justice and Virtue,
the mere existence of the words shows that the people,
as a whole, possessed a moral sense, and felt that certain
things were right and others wrong. What the moralist
did was to show the connection between different virtues,
the likeness of virtue to certain other things, the implications which a thoughtful man could find in the common
language. Wherever the Greek moral sense had come
from, it was there in the people before it could be enforced
by a prophet or discussed by a philosopher. Again,
we find a wonderful collection of moral aphorisms in
those shrewd sayings of the Jewish fathers which are
preserved in the Mishna or oral law. Some of this
teaching is familiar to us all from the popular exposition
of it which is contained in the three first Gospels. But
the very plainness and homeliness of the precepts shows
that they are just acute statements of what was already
felt by the popular common sense; protesting, in many
cases, against the formalism of the ceremonial law with
which they are curiously mixed up. The Rabbis even
show a jealousy of prophetic interference, as if they knew

well that it takes not one man, but many men, to feel
what is right. When a certain Rabbi Eliezer, being
worsted in argument, cried out, " If I am right, let
heaven pronounce in my favour! " there was heard a
Bath-kol or voice from the skies, saying " Do you
venture to dispute with Rabbi Eliezer, who is an authority
on all religious questions? " But Rabbi Joshua rose and
said, " Our law is not in heaven, but in the book which
dates from Sinai, and which teaches us that in matters of
discussion the majority makes the law." [1]

One of the most important expressions of the moral
sense for all time is that of the Stoic philosophy,
especially after its reception among the Romans. It
is here that we find the enthusiasm of humanity—the
caritas generis humani—which is so large and important
a feature in all modern conceptions of morality, and
whose widespread influence upon Roman citizens may
be traced in the Epistles of St. Paul. In the Stoic
emperors, also, we find probably the earliest example of
great moral principles consciously applied to legislation
on a large scale. But are we to attribute this to the
individual insight of the Stoic philosophers? It might
seem at first sight that we must, if we are to listen to that
vulgar vituperation of the older culture which has
descended to us from those who had everything to gain
by its destruction.[2] We hear enough of the luxurious
feasting of the Roman capital, how it would almost have
taxed the resources of a modern pastry-cook; of the

[1] Treatise Baba Bathra, 59 b. I derive this story and reference
from a most interesting book, " Kôl Kôre (Vox Clamantis), La Bible,
le Talmud, et l'Evangile; par le R. Elie Soloweyczyk. Paris:
E. Brière. 1870."

[2] Compare these passages from Merivale (Romans under the
Empire, vi.), to whom " it seems a duty to protect against the
common tendency of Christian moralists to dwell only on the dark
side of Pagan society, in order to heighten by contrast the blessings
of the Gospel " :—

" Much candour and discrimination are required in comparing
the sins of one age with those of another . . . the cruelty of our
inquisitions and sectarian persecutions, of our laws against sorcery,
our serfdom and our slavery; the petty fraudulence we tolerate in
almost every class and calling of the community; the bold front

cruelty of gladiatorial shows, how they were nearly as bad as *autos-da-fé*, except that a man had his fair chance, and was not tortured for torture's sake; of the oppression of provincials by people like Verres, of whom it may even be said that if they had been the East India Company they could not have been worse; of the complaints of Tacitus against bad and mad emperors (as Sir Henry Maine says); and of the still more serious complaints of the modern historian against the excessive taxation [1] which was one great cause of the fall of the empire. Of all this we are told a great deal; but we are not told of the many thousands of honourable men who carried civilisation to the ends of the known world, and administered a mighty empire so that it was loved and worshipped to the farthest corner of it. It is to these men and their common action that we must attribute the morality which found its organised expression in the writings of the Stoic philosophers. From these three cases we may gather that Right is a thing which must be done before it can be talked about, although after that it may only too easily be talked about without being done. Individual effort and energy may insist upon

---

worn by our open sensuality; the deeper degradation of that which is concealed; all these leave us little room for boasting of our modern discipline, and must deter the thoughtful inquirer from too confidently contrasting the morals of the old world and the new."

"Even at Rome, in the worst of times . . . all the relations of life were adorned in turn with bright instances of devotion, and mankind transacted their business with an ordinary confidence in the force of conscience and right reason. The steady development of enlightened legal principles conclusively proves the general dependence upon law as a guide and corrector of manners. In the camp, however, more especially, as the chief sphere of this purifying activity, the great qualities of the Roman character continued to be plainly manifested. This history of the Cæsars presents us to a constant succession of brave, patient, resolute, and faithful soldiers, men deeply impressed with a sense of duty, superior to vanity, despisers of boasting, content to toil in obscurity and shed their blood at the frontiers of the empire, unrepining at the cold mistrust of their masters, not clamorous for the honours so sparingly awarded to them, but satisfied in the daily work of their hands, and full of faith in the national destiny which they were daily accomplishing."

[1] Finlay, *Greece Under the Romans*.

getting that done which was already felt to be right; and individual insight and acumen may point out consequences of an action which bring it under previously known moral rules. There is another dispute of the Rabbis that may serve to show what is meant by this. It was forbidden by the law to have any dealings with the Sabæan idolaters during the week preceding their idolatrous feasts. But the doctors discussed the case in which one of these idolaters owes you a bill; are you to let him pay it during that week or not? The school of Shammai said " No; for he will want all his money to enjoy himself at the feast." But the school of Hillel said, " Yes, let him pay it; for how can he enjoy his feast while his bills are unpaid? " The question here is about the consequences of an action; but there is no dispute about the moral principle, which is that consideration and kindness are to be shown to idolaters, even in the matter of their idolatrous rites.

It seems, then, that we are no worse off than anybody else who has studied this subject, in finding our materials ready made for us; sufficiently definite meanings given in the common speech to the words " right " and " wrong," " good " and " bad," with which we have to deal; a fair body of facts familiarly known, which we have to organise and account for as best we can. But our special inquiry is, what account can be given of these facts by the scientific method? to which end we cannot do better than fix our ideas as well as we can upon the character and scope of that method.

Now the scientific method is a method of getting knowledge by inference, and that of two different kinds. One kind of inference is that which is used in the physical and natural sciences, and it enables us to go from known phenomena to unknown phenomena. Because a stone is heavy in the morning, I infer that it will be heavy in the afternoon; and I infer this by assuming a certain uniformity of nature. The sort of uniformity that I assume depends upon the extent of my scientific education; the rules of inference become more and more definite as we go on. At first I might assume that all things are always

alike; this would not be true, but it has to be assumed
in a vague way, in order that a thing may have the same
name at different times. Afterwards I get the more
definite belief that certain particular qualities, like weight,
have nothing to do with the time of day; and subsequently I find that weight has nothing to do with the
shape of the stone, but only with the quantity of it.
The uniformity which we assume, then, is not that vague
one that we started with, but a chastened and corrected
uniformity. I might go on to suppose, for example,
that the weight of the stone had nothing to do with the
place where it was; and a great deal might be said for
this supposition. It would, however, have to be corrected when it was found that the weight varies slightly
in different latitudes. On the other hand, I should find
that this variation was just the same for my stone as for
a piece of iron or wood; that it had nothing to do with
the kind of matter. And so I might be led to the conclusion that all matter is heavy, and that the weight of it
depends only on its quantity and its position relative to
the earth. You see here that I go on arriving at conclusions always of this form; that some one circumstance
or quality has nothing to do with some other circumstance or quality. I begin by assuming that it is independent of everything; I end by finding that it is independent of some definite things. That is, I begin by
assuming a vague uniformity. I always use this assumption to infer from some one fact a great number of other
facts; but as my education proceeds, I get to know what
sort of things may be inferred and what may not. An
observer of scientific mind takes note of just those things
from which inferences may be drawn, and passes by the
rest. If an astronomer, observing the sun, were to
record the fact that at the moment when a sun-spot began
to shrink there was a rap at his front door, we should
know that he was not up to his work. But if he records
that sun-spots are thickest every eleven years, and that
this is also the period of extra cloudiness in Jupiter, the
observation may or may not be confirmed, and it may
or may not lead to inferences of importance; but still

it is the kind of thing from which inferences may be drawn. There is always a certain instinct among instructed people which tells them in this way what kinds of inferences may be drawn ; and this is the unconscious effect of the definite uniformity which they have been led to assume in nature. It may subsequently be organised into a law or general truth, and no doubt becomes a surer guide by that process. Then it goes to form the more precise instinct of the next generation.

What we have said about this first kind of inference, which goes from phenomena to phenomena, is shortly this. It proceeds upon an assumption of uniformity in nature; and this assumption is not fixed and made once for all, but is a changing and growing thing, becoming more definite as we go on.

If I were told to pick out some one character which especially colours this guiding conception of uniformity in our present stage of science, I should certainly reply, Atomism. The form of this with which we are most familiar is the molecular theory of bodies; which represents all bodies as made up of small elements of uniform character, each practically having relations only with the adjacent ones, and these relations the same all through— namely, some simple mechanical action upon each other's motions. But this is only a particular case. A palace, a cottage, the tunnel of the underground railway, and a factory chimney, are all built of bricks; the bricks are alike in all these cases, each brick is practically related only to the adjacent ones, and the relation is throughout the same, namely, two flat sides are stuck together with mortar. There is an atomism in the sciences of number, of quantity, of space; the theorems of geometry are groupings of individual points, each related only to the adjacent ones by certain definite laws. But what concerns us chiefly at present is the atomism of human physiology. Just as every solid is built up of molecules, so the nervous system is built up of nerve-threads and nerve-corpuscles. We owe to Mr. Lewes our very best thanks for the stress which he has laid on the doctrine that nerve-fibre is uniform in structure and function, and for the word *neurility*, which expresses its common properties. And similar gratitude is due to Dr. Hughlings Jackson for his long defence of the proposition that the element of nervous structure and function is a sensori-motor process. In structure, this is two fibres or bundles of fibres going to the same gray corpuscle; in function it is a message travelling up one fibre or bundle to the corpuscle, and then down the other fibre or bundle.[1] Out of this, as a brick, the house of our life is built. All these simple elementary processes are alike, and each is practically related to only the adjacent ones; the relation being in all cases of the same kind, viz. the passage from a simple to a complex message, or *vice versa*.

The result of atomism in any form, dealing with any subject, is that the principle of uniformity is hunted down into the elements of things; it is resolved into the uniformity of these elements or atoms, and of the relations of those which are next to each other. By an element or an atom we do not here mean something absolutely simple or indivisible, for a molecule, a brick, and a nerve-process are all very complex things. We only mean that, for the purpose in hand, the properties of the still more complex thing which is made of them have nothing to do with the complexities or the differences of these elements. The solid made of molecules, the house made of bricks, the nervous system made of sensori-motor processes, are nothing more than collections of these practically uniform elements, having certain relations of nextness, and behaviour uniformly depending on that nextness.

The inference of phenomena from phenomena, then, is based upon an assumption of uniformity, which in the present stage of science may be called an atomic uniformity.

The other mode of inference which belongs to the scientific method is that which is used in what are called

[1] Mr. Herbert Spencer had assigned a slightly different element. —*Principles of Psychology*, vol. i. p. 28.

the mental and moral sciences; and it enables us to go from phenomena to the facts which underlie phenomena, and which are themselves not phenomena at all. If I pinch your arm, and you draw it away and make a face, I infer that you have felt pain. I infer this by assuming that you have a consciousness similar to my own, and related to your perception of your body as my consciousness is related to my perception of my body. Now is this the same assumption as before, a mere assumption of the uniformity of nature? It certainly seems like it at first; but if we think about it we shall find that there is a very profound difference between them. In physical inference I go from phenomena to phenomena; that is, from the knowledge of certain appearances or representations actually present to my mind I infer certain other appearances that might be present to my mind. From the weight of a stone in the morning— that is, from my feeling of its weight, or my perception of the process of weighing it, I infer that the stone will be heavy in the afternoon—that is, I infer the possibility of similar feelings and perceptions in me at another time. The whole process relates to me and my perceptions, to things contained in my mind. But when I infer that you are conscious from what you say or do, I pass from that which is *my* feeling or perception, which is in my mind and part of me, to that which is not my feeling at all, which is outside me altogether, namely, *your* feelings and perceptions. Now there is no possible physical inference, no inference of phenomena from phenomena, that will help me over that gulf. I am obliged to admit that this second kind of inference depends upon another assumption, not included in the assumption of the uniformity of phenomena.

How does a dream differ from waking life? In a fairly coherent dream everything seems quite real, and it is rare, I think, with most people to know in a dream that they are dreaming. Now, if a dream is sufficiently vivid and coherent, all physical inferences are just as valid in it as they are in waking life. In a hazy or imperfect dream, it is true, things melt into one another unexpectedly and unaccountably; we fly, remove mountains, and stop runaway horses with a finger. But there is nothing in the mere nature of a dream to hinder it from being an exact copy of waking experience. If I find a stone heavy in one part of my dream, and infer that it is heavy at some subsequent part, the inference will be verified if the dream is coherent enough; I shall go to the stone, lift it up, and find it as heavy as before. And the same thing is true of all inferences of phenomena from phenomena. For physical purposes a dream is just as good as real life; the only difference is in vividness and coherence.

What, then, hinders us from saying that life is all a dream? If the phenomena we dream of are just as good and real phenomena as those we see and feel when we are awake, what right have we to say that the material universe has any more existence apart from our minds than the things we see and feel in our dreams? The answer which Berkeley gave to that question was, No right at all. The physical universe which I see, and feel, and infer, is just my dream and nothing else; that which you see is your dream; only it so happens that all our dreams agree in many respects. This doctrine of Berkeley's has now been so far confirmed by the physiology of the senses that it is no longer a metaphysical speculation, but a scientifically established fact.

But there is a difference between dreams and waking life which is of far too great importance for any of us to be in danger of neglecting it. When I see a man in my dream there is just as good a *body* as if I were awake; muscles, nerves, circulation, capability of adapting means to ends. If only the dream is coherent enough, no physical test can establish that it is a dream. In both cases I see and feel the same thing. In both cases I assume the existence of more than I can see and feel, namely, the consciousness of this other man. But now here is a great difference, and the only difference—in a dream this assumption is wrong; in waking life it is right. The man I see in my dream is a *mere* machine, a bundle of phenomena with no underlying reality; there is no consciousness involved except my consciousness, no feeling in the case except my feelings. The man I see in waking life is more than a bundle of phenomena; his body and its actions are phenomena, but these phenomena are merely the symbols and representatives in my mind of a reality which is outside my mind, namely, the consciousness of the man himself which is represented by the working of his brain, and the simpler quasi-mental facts, not woven into his consciousness, which are represented by the working of the rest of his body. What makes life not to be a dream is the existence of those facts which we arrive at by our second process of inference ; the consciousness of men and the higher animals, the sub-consciousness of lower organisms, and the quasi-mental facts which go along with the motions of inanimate matter. In a book which is very largely and deservedly known by heart, *Through the Looking-glass*, there is a very instructive discussion upon this point. Alice has been taken to see the Red King as he lies snoring; and Tweedledee asks, " Do you know what he is dreaming about? " " Nobody can guess that," replies Alice. " Why, about *you*," he says triumphantly. " And if he stopped dreaming about you, where do you suppose you'd be? " " Where I am now, of course," said Alice. " Not you," said Tweedledee, " you'd be nowhere. You are only a sort of thing in his dream." " If that there King was to wake," added Tweedledum, " you'd go out, bang! just like a candle." Alice was quite right in regarding these remarks as unphilosophical. The fact that she could see, think, and feel, was proof positive that she was not a sort of thing in anybody's dream. This is the meaning of that saying, *Cogito ergo sum*, of Descartes. By him, and by Spinoza after him, the verb *cogito* and the substantive *cogitatio* were used to denote consciousness in general, any kind of feeling, even what we now call subconsciousness. The saying means that feeling exists in and for itself, not as a quality or modification or state of manifestation of anything else.

We are obliged in every hour of our lives to act upon

beliefs which have been arrived at by inferences of these
two kinds; inferences based on the assumption f
uniformity in nature, and inferences which add to this
the assumption of feelings which are not our own. By
organising the " common sense " which embodies the
first class of inferences, we build up the physical sciences;
that is to say, all those sciences which deal with the
physical, material, or phenomenal universe, whether
animate or inanimate. And so by organising the
common sense which embodies the second class of
inferences, we build up various sciences of mind. The
description and classification of feelings, the facts of
their association with each other, and of their simultaneity
with phenomena of nerve-action—all this belongs to
psychology, which may be historical and comparative.
The doctrine of certain special classes of feelings is
organised into the special sciences of those feelings; thus
the facts about the feelings which we are now considering, about the feelings of moral approbation and reprobation, are organised into the science of ethics, and the facts
about the feeling of beauty or ugliness are organised into
the science of æsthetics, or, as it is sometimes called,
the philosophy of art. For all of these the uniformity
of nature has to be assumed as a basis of inference; but
over and above that it is necessary to assume that other
men are conscious in the same way that I am. Now in
these sciences of mind, just as in the physical sciences,
the uniformity which is assumed in the inferred mental
facts is a growing thing which becomes more definite as
we go on, and each successive generation of observers
knows better what to observe and what sort of inferences
may be drawn from observed things. But, moreover,
it is as true of the mental sciences as of the physical
ones that the uniformity is in the present stage of science
an *atomic* uniformity. We have learned to regard our
consciousness as made up of elements practically alike,
having relations of succession in time and of contiguity
at each instant, which relations are in all cases practically
the same. The element of consciousness is the trans-
ference of an impression into the beginning of action.

Our mental life is a structure made out of such elements, just as the working of our nervous system is made out of sensori-motor processes.   And accordingly the inter-action of the two branches of science leads us to regard the mental facts as the realities or things-in-themselves, of which the material phenomena are mere pictures or symbols.   The final result seems to be that atomism is carried beyond phenomena into the realities which phenomena represent; and that the observed uniformities of nature, in so far as they can be expressed in the lan-guage of atomism, are actual uniformities of things in themselves.

So much for the two things which I have promised to bring together; the facts of our moral feelings, and the scientific method.   It may appear that the latter has been expounded at more length than was necessary for the treatment of this particular subject; but the justifica-tion for this length is to be found in certain common objections to the claims of science to be the sole judge of mental and moral questions.   Some of the chief of these objections I will now mention.

It is sometimes said that science can only deal with what is, but that art and morals deal with what ought to be.   The saying is perfectly true, but it is quite consistent with what is equally true, that the facts of art and morals are fit subject-matter of science.   I may describe all that I have in my house, and I may state everything that I want in my house; these are two very different things, but they are equally statements of facts. One is a statement about phenomena, about the objects which are actually in my possession; the other is a statement about my feelings, about my wants and desires. There are facts, to be got at by common sense, about the kind of thing that a man of a certain character and occupation will like to have in his house, and these facts may be organised into general statements on the assump-tion of uniformity in nature.   Now the organised results of common sense dealing with facts are just science and nothing else.   And in the same way I may say what men do at the present day, how we live now, or I may say what we ought to do, namely, what course of conduct, if adopted, we should morally approve; and no doubt these would be two very different things. But each of them would be a statement of facts. One would belong to the sociology of our time; in so far as men's deeds could not be adequately described to us without some account of their feelings and intentions, it would involve facts belonging to psychology as well as facts belonging to the physical sciences. But the other would be an account of a particular class of our feelings, namely, those which we feel towards an action when it is regarded as right or wrong. These facts may be organised by common sense on the assumption of uniformity in nature just as well as any other facts. And we shall see farther on that not only in this sense, but in a deeper and more abstract sense, " what ought to be done " is a question for scientific inquiry.

The same objection is sometimes put into another form. It is said that laws of chemistry, for example, are general statements about what happens when bodies are treated in a certain way, and that such laws are fit matter for science; but that moral laws are different, because they tell us to do certain things, and we may or may not obey them. The mood of the one is indicative, of the other imperative. Now it is quite true that the word *law* in the expression " law of nature," and in the expressions " law of morals," " law of the land," has two totally different meanings, which no educated person will confound; and I am not aware that anyone has rested the claim of science to judge moral questions on what is no better than a stale and unprofitable pun. But two different things may be equally matters of scientific investigation, even when their names are alike in sound. A telegraph post is not the same thing as a post in the War Office, and yet the same intelligence may be used to investigate the conditions of the one and the other. That such and such things are right or wrong, that such and such laws are laws of morals or laws of the land, these are facts, just as the laws of chemistry are facts; and all facts belong to science, and are her portion for ever.

Again, it is sometimes said that moral questions have

been authoritatively settled by other methods; that we ought to accept this decision, and not to question it by any method of scientific inquiry; and that reason should give way to revelation on such matters. I hope before I have done to show just cause why we should pronounce on such teachings as this no light sentence of moral condemnation; first, because it is our duty to form those beliefs which are to guide our actions by the two scientific modes of inference, and by these alone; and, secondly, because the proposed mode of settling ethical questions by authority is contrary to the very nature of right and wrong.

Leaving this, then, for the present, I pass on to the most formidable objection that has been made to a scientific treatment of ethics. The objection is that the scientific method is not applicable to human action, because the rule of uniformity does not hold good. Whenever a man exercises his will, and makes a voluntary choice of one out of various possible courses, an event occurs whose relation to contiguous events cannot be included in a general statement applicable to all similar cases. There is something wholly capricious and disorderly, belonging to that moment only; and we have no right to conclude that if the circumstances were exactly repeated, and the man himself absolutely unaltered, he would choose the same course.

It is clear that if the doctrine here stated is true, the ground is really cut from under our feet, and we cannot deal with human action by the scientific method. I shall endeavour to show, moreover, that in this case, although we might still have a feeling of moral approbation or reprobation towards actions, yet we could not reasonably praise or blame men for their deeds, nor regard them - as morally responsible. So that if my contention is just, to deprive us of the scientific method is practically to deprive us of morals altogether. On both grounds, therefore, it is of the greatest importance that we should define our position in regard to this controversy; if, indeed, that can be called a controversy in which the practical belief of all mankind and the consent of nearly all serious writers are on one s de.

Let us in the first place consider a little more closely the connection between conscience and responsibility. Words in common use, such as these two, have their meanings practically fixed before difficult controversies arise; but after the controversy has arisen, each party gives that slight tinge to the meaning which best suits its own view of the question. Thus it appears to each that the common language obviously supports their own view, that this is the natural and primary view of the matter, and that the opponents are using words in a new meaning and wresting them from their proper sense. Now this is just my position. I have endeavoured so far to use all words in their common everyday sense, only making this as precise as I can; and, with two exceptions, of which due warning will be given, I shall do my best to continue this practice in future. I seem to myself to be talking the most obvious platitudes; but it must be remembered that those who take the opposite view will think I am perverting the English language.

There is a common meaning of the word " responsible," which, though not the same as that of the phrase " morally responsible," may throw some light upon it. If we say of a book, " A is responsible for the preface and the first half, and B is responsible for the rest," we mean that A wrote the preface and the first half. If two people go into a shop and choose a blue silk dress together, it might be said that A was responsible for its being silk and B for its being blue. Before they chose, the dress was undetermined both in colour and in material. A's choice fixed the material, and then it was undetermined only in colour. B's choice fixed the colour; and if we suppose that there were no more variable conditions (only one blue silk dress in the shop), the dress was then completely determined. In this sense of the word we say that a man is responsible for that part of an event which was undetermined when he was left out of account, and which became determined when he was taken account of. Suppose two narrow streets, one lying north and south, one east and west, and crossing one another. A man is put down where they cross, and has to walk. Then he must walk either north, south, east, or west, and he is not responsible for that; what he is responsible for is the choice of one of these four directions. May we not say in the present sense of the word that the external circumstances are responsible for the restriction on his choice? We should mean only that the fact of his going in one or other of the four directions was due to external circumstances and not to him. Again, suppose I have a number of punches of various shapes, some square, some oblong, some oval, some round, and that I am going to punch a hole in a piece of paper. *Where* I shall punch the hole may be fixed by any kind of circumstances; but the shape of the hole depends on the punch I take. May we not say that the punch is responsible for the shape of the hole, but not for the position of it?

It may be said that this is not the whole of the meaning of the word " responsible," even in its loosest sense; that it ought never to be used except of a conscious agent. Still this is part of its meaning; if we regard an event as determined by a variety of circumstances, a man's choice being among them, we say that he is responsible for just that choice which is left him by the other circumstances.

When we ask the practical question, " Who is responsible for so-and-so? " we want to find out who is to be got at in order that so-and-so may be altered. If I want to change the shape of the hole I make in my paper, I must change my punch; but this will be of no use if I want to change the position of the hole. If I want the colour of the dress changed from blue to green, it is B, and not A, that I must persuade.

We mean something more than this when we say that a man is *morally* responsible for an action. It seems to me that moral responsibility and conscience go together, both in regard to the man and in regard to the action. In order that a man may be morally responsible for an action, the man must have a conscience, and the action must be one in regard to which conscience is capable of acting as a motive, that is, the action must be capable of being right or wrong. If a child were left on a desert island and grew up wholly without a conscience, and then were brought among men, he would not be morally responsible for his actions until he had acquired a conscience by education. He would of course be *responsible*, in the sense just explained, for that part of them which was left undetermined by external circumstances, and if we wanted to alter his actions in these respects we should have to do it by altering him. But it would be useless and unreasonable to attempt to do this by means of praise or blame, the expression of moral approbation or disapprobation; until he had acquired a conscience which could be worked upon by such means.

It seems, then, that in order that a man may be morally responsible for an action, three things are necessary:—

1. He might have done something else; that is to say, the action was not wholly determined by external circumstances, and he is responsible only for the choice which was left him.

2. He had a conscience.

3. The action was one in regard to the doing or not doing of which conscience might be a sufficient motive.

These three things are necessary, but it does not follow that they are sufficient. It is very commonly said that the action must be a *voluntary* one. It will be found, I think, that this is contained in my third condition, and also that the form of statement I have adopted exhibits more clearly the reason why the condition is necessary. We may say that an action is involuntary either when it is instinctive, or when one motive is so strong that there is no voluntary choice between motives. An involuntary cough produced by irritation of the glottis is no proper subject for blame or praise. A man is not responsible for it, because it is done by a part of his body without consulting *him*. What is meant by *him* in this case will require further investigation. Again, when a dipsomaniac has so great and overmastering an inclination to drink that we cannot conceive of conscience being strong enough to conquer it, he is not responsible for that act, though he may be responsible for having got himself into the state. But if it is conceivable that a very strong conscience fully brought to bear might succeed in conquering the inclination, we may take a lenient view of the fall and say there was a very strong temptation, but we shall still regard it as a fall, and say that the man is responsible and a wrong has been done.[1]

But since it is just in this distinction between voluntary and involuntary action that the whole *crux* of the matter lies, let us examine more closely into it. I say that when I cough or sneeze involuntarily, it is really not I that cough or sneeze, but a part of my body which acts without consulting me. This action is determined for me by the circumstances, and is not part of the choice that is left to me, so that I am not responsible for it. The question comes then to determining how much is to be called *circumstances*, and how much is to be called *me*.

Now I want to describe what happens when I voluntarily do anything, and there are two courses open to me. I may describe the things in themselves, my feelings and the general course of my consciousness, trusting to the analogy between my consciousness and yours to make me understood; or I may describe these things as nature describes them to your senses, namely, in terms of the phenomena, of my nervous system, appealing to your memory of phenomena and your knowledge of physical action. I shall do both, because in some respects our knowledge is more complete from the one source, and in some respects from the other. When I look back and reflect upon a voluntary action, I seem to find that it differs from an involuntary action in the fact that a certain portion of my character has been consulted. There is always a suggestion of some sort,

[1] [It seems worth noting that this very closely coincides with the doctrine of modern English law on the questions when and how far insanity excludes criminal responsibility.]

either the end of a train of thought or a new sensation; and there is an action ensuing, either the movement of a muscle or set of muscles, or the fixing of attention upon something. But between these two there is a consultation, as it were, of my past history. The suggestion is viewed in the light of everything bearing on it that I think of at the time, and in virtue of this light it moves me to act in one or more ways. Let us first suppose that no hesitation is involved, that only one way of acting is suggested, and I yield to this impulse and act in the particular way. This is the simplest kind of voluntary action. It differs from involuntary or instinctive action in the fact that with the latter there is no such conscious consultation of past history. If we describe these facts in terms of the phenomena which picture them to other minds, we shall say that in involuntary action a message passes straight through from the sensory to the motor centre, and so on to the muscles, without consulting the cerebrum; while in voluntary action the message is passed on from the sensory centre to the cerebrum, there translated into appropriate motor stimuli, carried down to the motor centre, and so on to the muscles. There may be other differences, but at least there is this difference. Now, on the physical side, that which determines what groups of cerebral fibres shall be set at work by the given message, and what groups of motor stimuli shall be set at work by these, is the mechanism of my brain at the time; and on the mental side, that which determines what memories shall be called up by the given sensation, and what motives these memories shall bring into action, is my mental character. We may say, then, in this simplest case of voluntary action, that when the suggestion is given, it is the character of *me* which determines the character of the ensuing action; and consequently that I am responsible for choosing that particular course out of those which were left open to me by the external cirumstances.

This is when I yield to the impulse. But suppose I do not; suppose that the original suggestion, viewed in the light of memory, sets various motives in action, each motive belonging to a certain class of things which I remember. Then I choose which of these motives shall prevail. Those who carefully watch themselves find out that a particular motive is made to prevail by the fixing of the attention upon that class of remembered things which calls up the motive. The physical side of this is the sending of blood to a certain set of nerves—namely, those whose action corresponds to the memories which are to be attended to. The sending of blood is accomplished by the pinching of arteries; and there are special nerves, called vaso-motor nerves, whose business it is to carry messages to the walls of the arteries and get them pinched. Now this act of directing the attention may be voluntary or involuntary, just like any other act. When the transformed and reinforced nerve-message gets to the vaso-motor centre, some part of it may be so predominant that a message goes straight off to the arteries, and sends a quantity of blood to the nerves supplying that part; or the call for blood may be sent back for revision by the cerebrum, which is thus again consulted. To say the same thing in terms of my feelings, a particular class of memories roused by the original suggestion may seize upon my attention before I have time to choose what I will attend to; or the appeal may be carried to a deeper part of my character dealing with wider and more abstract conceptions, which views the conflicting motives in the light of a past experience of motives, and by that light is drawn to one or the other of them.

We thus get to a sort of motive of the second order or motives of motives. Is there any reason why we should not go on to a motive of the third order, and the fourth, and so on? None whatever that I know of, except that no one has ever observed such a thing. There seems plenty of room for the requisite mechanism on the physical side; and no one can say, on the mental side, how complex is the working of his consciousness. But we must carefully distinguish between the intellectual deliberation about motives, which applies to the future and the past, and the practical choice of motives in the moment of will. The former may be a train of any

length and complexity: we have no reason to believe
that the latter is more than engine and tender.

We are now in a position to classify actions in respect
of the kind of responsibility which belongs to them;
namely, we have—

1. Involuntary or instinctive actions.
2. Voluntary actions in which the choice of motives is
involuntary.
3. Voluntary actions in which the choice of motives is
voluntary.

In each of these cases what is responsible is that part
of my character which determines what the action shall
be. For instinctive actions we do not say that *I* am
responsible, because the choice is made before I know
anything about it. For voluntary actions I am responsible, because I make the choice; that is, the
character of me is what determines the character of the
action. In *me*, then, for this purpose, is included the
aggregate of links of association which determines what
memories shall be called up by a given suggestion, and
what motives shall be set at work by these memories.
But we distinguish this mass of passions and pleasures,
desire and knowledge and pain, which makes up most of
my character at the moment, from that inner and deeper
motive-choosing self which is called Reason, and the
Will, and the Ego; which is only responsible when
motives are voluntarily chosen by directing attention to
them. It is responsible only for the choice of one motive
out of those presented to it, not for the nature of the
motives which are presented.

But again, I may reasonably be blamed for what I did
yesterday, or a week ago, or last year. This is because
I am permanent; in so far as from my actions of that
date an inference may be drawn about my character now,
it is reasonable that I should be treated as praiseworthy
or blamable. And within certain limits I am for the
same reason responsible for what I am now, because
within certain limits I have made myself. Even instinctive actions are dependent in many cases upon habits

which may be altered by proper attention and care; and still more the nature of the connections between sensation and action, the associations of memory and motive, may be voluntarily modified if I choose to try. The habit of choosing among motives is one which may be acquired and strengthened by practice, and the strength of particular motives, by continually directing attention to them, may be almost indefinitely increased or diminished. Thus, if by *me* is meant not the instantaneous me of this moment, but the aggregate me of my past life, or even of the last year, the range of my responsibility is very largely increased. I am responsible for a very large portion of the circumstances which are now external to me; that is to say, I am responsible for certain of the restrictions on my own freedom. As the eagle was shot with an arrow that flew on its own feather, so I find myself bound with fetters of my proper forging.

Let us now endeavour to conceive an action which is not determined in any way by the character of the agent. If we ask, " What makes it to be that action and no other? " we are told, " The man's Ego." The words are here used, it seems to me, in some non-natural sense, if in any sense at all. One thing makes another to be what it is when the characters of the two things are connected together by some general statement or rule. But we have to suppose that the character of the action is not connected with the character of the Ego by any general statement or rule. With the same Ego and the same circumstances of all kinds, anything within the limits imposed by the cirumstances may happen at any moment. I find myself unable to conceive any distinct sense in which responsibility could apply in this case; nor do I see at all how it would be reasonable to use praise or blame. If the action does not depend on the character, what is the use of trying to alter the character? Suppose, however, that this indeterminateness is only partial; that the character does add some restrictions to those already imposed by circumstances, but leaves the choice between certain actions undetermined, and to be settled by chance or the transcendental Ego. Is it not clear that the man would be responsible for precisely that part of the character of the action which was determined by his character, and not for what was left undetermined by it? For it is just that part which was determined by his character which it is reasonable to try to alter by altering him.

We who believe in uniformity are not the only people unable to conceive responsibility without it. These are the words of Sir W. Hamilton, as quoted by Mr. J. S. Mill [1]:—

" Nay, were we even to admit as true what we cannot think as possible, still the doctrine of a motiveless volition would be only casualism; and the free acts of an indifferent are, morally and rationally, as worthless as the pre-ordered passions of a determined will."

" That, though inconceivable, a motiveless volition would, if conceived, be conceived as morally worthless, only shows our impotence more clearly."

" Is the person an *original undetermined* cause of the determination of his will? If he be not, then he is not a *free agent*, and the scheme of Necessity is admitted. If he be, in the first place, it is impossible to *conceive* the possibility of this; and in the second, if the fact, though inconceivable, be allowed, it is impossible to see how a cause, undetermined by any motive, can be a rational, moral, and accountable cause."

It is true that Hamilton also says that the scheme of necessity is inconceivable, because it leads to an infinite non-commencement; and that " the possibility of morality depends on the possibility of liberty; for if a man be not a free agent, he is not the author of his actions, and has therefore no responsibility—no moral personality at all."

I know nothing about necessity; I only believe that nature is practically uniform even in human action. I know nothing about an infinitely distant past; I only know that I ought to base on uniformity those inferences which are to guide my actions. But that man is a free

[1] *Examination*, p. 495, 2nd ed.

agent appears to me obvious, and that in the natural sense of the words. We need ask for no better definition than Kant's :—

" Will is a kind of causality belonging to living agents, in so far as they are rational; and freedom is such a property of that causality as enables them to be efficient agents independently of outside causes determining them; as, on the other hand, necessity (*Naturnothwendigkeit*) is that property of all irrational beings which consists in their being determined to activity by the influence of outside causes."

I believe that I am a free agent when my actions are independent of the control of circumstances outside me; and it seems a misuse of language to call me a free agent if my actions are determined by a transcendental Ego who is independent of the circumstances inside me—that is to say, of my character. The expression "free will" has unfortunately been imported into mental science from a theological controversy rather different from the one we are now considering. It is surely too much to expect that good and serviceable English words should be sacrificed to a phantom.

In an admirable book, *The Methods of Ethics*, Mr. Henry Sidgwick has stated, with supreme fairness and impartiality, both sides of this question. After setting forth the "almost overwhelming cumulative proof" of uniformity in human action, he says that it seems "more than balanced by a single argument on the other side: the immediate affirmation of consciousness in the moment of deliberate volition." "No amount of experience of the sway of motives ever tends to make me distrust my intuitive consciousness that in resolving, after deliberation, I exercise free choice as to which of the motives acting upon me shall prevail."

The only answer to this argument is that it is not "on the other side." There is no doubt about the deliverance of consciousness; and even if our powers of self-observation had not been acute enough to discover it, the

[1] *Metaphysics of Ethics*, chap. iii.

existence of some choice between motives would be
proved by the existence of vaso-motor nerves. But
perhaps the most instructive way of meeting arguments
of this kind is to inquire what consciousness ought to
say in order that its deliverances may be of any use in the
controversy. It is affirmed, on the side of uniformity, that
the feelings in my consciousness in the moment of voluntary choice have been preceded by facts out of my consciousness which are related to them in a uniform manner,
so that if the previous facts had been accurately known
the voluntary choice might have been predicted. On the
other side this is denied. To be of any use in the controversy, then, the immediate deliverance of my consciousness must be competent to assure me of the non-
existence of something which by hypothesis is not in my
consciousness. Given an absolutely dark room, can my
sense of sight assure me that there is no one but myself
in it? Can my sense of hearing assure me that nothing
inaudible is going on? As little can the immediate
deliverance of my consciousness assure me that the
uniformity of nature does not apply to human actions.

It is perhaps necessary, in connection with this
question, to refer to that singular Materialism of high
authority and recent date which makes consciousness a
physical agent, " correlates " it with Light and Nerve-
force, and so reduces it to an objective phenomenon.
This doctrine is founded on a common and very useful
mode of speech, in which we say, for example, that a good
fire is a source of pleasure on a cold day, and that a man's
feeling of chill may make him run to it. But so also we
say that the sun rises and sets every morning and night,
although the man in the moon sees clearly that this is
due to the rotation of the earth. One cannot be pedantic
all day. But if we choose for once to be pedantic, the
matter is after all very simple. Suppose that I am made
to run by feeling a chill. When I begin to move my leg,
I may observe if I like a double series of facts. I have
the feeling of effort, the sensation of motion in my leg;
I feel the pressure of my foot on the ground. Along with
this I may see with my eyes, or feel with my hands, the

motion of my leg as a material object.   The first series
of facts belongs to me alone; the second may be equally
observed by anybody else.   The mental series began first ;
I willed to move my leg before I saw it move.   But when
I know more about the matter, I can trace the material
series farther back, and find nerve-messages going to the
muscles of my leg to make it move.   But I had a feeling
of chill before I chose to move my leg.   Accordingly, I
can find nerve-messages, excited by the contraction due
to the low temperature, going to my brain from the
chilled skin.   Assuming the uniformity of nature, I carry
forward and backward both the mental and the material
series.   A uniformity is observed in each, and a parallel-
ism is observed between them, whenever observations
can be made.   But sometimes one series is known better,
and sometimes the other;   so that in telling a story we
quite naturally speak sometimes of mental facts and sometimes of material facts.   A feeling of chill made a man
run;   strictly speaking, the nervous disturbance which
coexisted with that feeling of chill made him run, if we
want to talk about material facts;   or the feeling of chill
produced the form of sub-consciousness which coexists
with the motion of legs, if we want to talk about mental
facts.   But we know nothing about the special nervous
disturbance which coexists with a feeling of chill, because
it has not yet been localised in the brain;   and we know
nothing about the form of sub-consciousness which
coexists with the motion of legs;   although there is very
good reason for believing in the existence of both.   So
we talk about the feeling of chill and the running, because
in one case we know the mental side, and in the other the
material side.   A man might show me a picture of the
battle of Gravelotte, and say: " You can't see the battle,
because it's all over, but there is a picture of it."   And
then he might put a chassepot into my hand, and say :
" We could not represent the whole construction of a
chassepot in the picture, but you can examine this one,
and find it out."   If I now insisted on mixing up the two
modes of communication of knowledge, if I expected
that the chassepots in the picture would go off, and said

that the one in my hand was painted on heavy canvas, I should be acting exactly in the spirit of the new materialism. For the material facts are a representation or symbol of the mental facts, just as a picture is a representation or symbol of a battle. And my own mind is a reality from which I can judge by analogy of the realities represented by other men's brains, just as the chassepot in my hand is a reality from which I can judge by analogy of the chassepots represented in the picture. When, therefore, we ask, " What is the physical link between the ingoing message from chilled skin and the outgoing message which moves the leg?" and the answer is, " A man's Will," we have as much right to be amused as if we had asked our friend with the picture what pigment was used in painting the cannon in the foreground, and received the answer, " Wrought iron." It will be found excellent practice in the mental operations required by this doctrine to imagine a train, the fore part of which is an engine and three carriages linked with iron couplings, and the hind part three other carriages linked with iron couplings; the bond between the two parts being made out of the sentiments of amity subsisting between the stoker and the guard.

To sum up: the uniformity of nature in human actions has been denied on the ground that it takes away responsibility, that it is contradicted by the testimony of consciousness, and that there is a physical correlation between mind and matter. We have replied that the uniformity of nature is necessary to responsibility, that it is affirmed by the testimony of consciousness whenever consciousness is competent to testify, and that matter is the phenomenon or symbol of which mind or quasi-mind is the symbolised and represented thing. We are now free to continue our inquiries on the supposition that nature is uniform.

We began by describing the moral sense of an Englishman. No doubt the description would serve very well for the more civilised nations of Europe; most closely for Germans and Dutch. But the fact that we can speak in this way discloses that there is more than one moral sense, and that what I feel to be right another man may feel to be wrong. Thus we cannot help asking whether there is any reason for preferring one moral sense to another; whether the question, " What is right to do? " has in any one set of circumstances a single answer which can be definitely known.

Clearly, in the first rough sense of the word, this is not true. What is right for me to do now, seeing that I am here with a certain character, and a certain moral sense as part of it, is just what I feel to be right. The individual conscience is, in the moment of volition, the only possible judge of what is right; there is no conflicting claim. But if we are deliberating about the future, we know that we can modify our conscience gradually by associating with people, reading certain books, and paying attention to certain ideas and feelings; and we may ask ourselves, " How shall we modify our conscience, if at all? what kind of conscience shall we try to get? what is the *best* conscience? " We may ask similar questions about our sense of taste. There is no doubt at present that the nicest things to me are the things I like; but I know that I can train myself to like some things and dislike others, and that things which are very nasty at one time may come to be great delicacies at another. I may ask, " How shall I train myself? What is the *best* taste? " And this leads very naturally to putting the question in another form, namely, " What is taste good for? What is the *purpose* or *function* of taste? " We should probably find as the answer to that question that the purpose or function of taste is to discriminate wholesome food from unwholesome; that it is a matter of stomach and digestion. It will follow from this that the best taste is that which prefers wholesome food, and that by cultivating a preference for wholesome and nutritious things I shall be training my palate in the way it should go. In just the same way our question about the best conscience will resolve itself into a question about the purpose or function of the conscience—why we have got it, and what it is good for.

Now to my mind the simplest and clearest and most

profound philosophy that was ever written upon this subject is to be found in the 2nd and 3rd chapters of Mr. Darwin's *Descent of Man*. In these chapters it appears that just as most physical characteristics of organisms have been evolved and preserved because they were useful to the individual in the struggle for existence against other individuals and other species, so this particular feeling has been evolved and preserved because it is useful to the tribe or community in the struggle for existence against other tribes, and against the environment as a whole. The function of conscience is the preservation of the tribe as a tribe. And we shall rightly train our consciences if we learn to approve those actions which tend to the advantage of the community in the struggle for existence.

There are here some words, however, which require careful definition. And first the word *purpose*. A thing serves a purpose when it is adapted to some end; thus a corkscrew is adapted to the end of extracting corks from bottles, and our lungs are adapted to the end of respiration. We may say that the extraction of corks is the purpose of the corkscrew, and that respiration is the purpose of the lungs. But here we shall have used the word in two different senses. A man made the corkscrew with a purpose in his mind, and he knew and intended that it should be used for pulling out corks. But nobody made our lungs with a purpose in his mind, and intended that they should be used for breathing. The respiratory apparatus was adapted to its purpose by natural selection—namely, by the gradual preservation of better and better adaptations, and the killing off of the worse and imperfect adaptations. In using the word " purpose " for the result of this unconscious process of adaptation by survival of the fittest, I know that I am somewhat extending its ordinary sense, which implies consciousness. But it seems to me that on the score of convenience there is a great deal to be said for this extension of meaning. We want a word to express the adptation of means to an end, whether involving consciousness or not; the word " purpose " will do very well, and the adjective *purposive* has already been used in this sense.   But if the use is admitted, we must distinguish two kinds of purpose.   There is the unconscious purpose which is attained by natural selection, in which no consciousness need be concerned;   and there is the conscious purpose of an intelligence which designs a thing that it may serve to do something which he desires to be done.   The distinguishing mark of this second kind, design or conscious purpose, is that in the consciousness of the agent there is an image or symbol of the end which he desires, and this precedes and determines the use of the means.   Thus the man who first invented a corkscrew must have previously known that corks were in bottles, and have desired to get them out. We may describe this if we like in terms of matter, and say that a purpose of the second kind implies a complex nervous system, in which there can be formed an image or symbol of the end, and that this symbol determines the use of the means.   The nervous image or symbol of anything is that mode of working of part of my brain which goes on simultaneously and is correlated with my thinking of the thing.

Aristotle defines an organism as that in which the part exists for the sake of the whole.   It is not that the existence of the part depends on the existence of the whole, for every whole exists only as an aggregate of parts related in a certain way;   but that the shape and nature of the part are determined by the wants of the whole.   Thus the shape and nature of my foot are what they are, not for the sake of my foot itself, but for the sake of my whole body, and because it wants to move about.   That which the part has to do for the whole is called its function.   Thus the function of my foot is to support me, and assist in locomotion.   Not all the nature of the part is necessarily for the sake of the whole : the comparative callosity of the skin of my sole is for the protection of my foot itself.

Society is an organism, and man in society is part of an organism according to this definition, in so far as some portion of the nature of man is what it is for the sake of

the whole—society. . Now conscience is such a portion of
the nature of man, and its function is the preservation of
society in the struggle for existence.   We may be able to
define this function more closely when we know more
about the way in which conscience tends to preserve
society.

Next let us endeavour to make precise the meaning of
the words *community* and *society*.   It is clear that at
different times men may be divided into groups of greater
or less extent—tribes, clans, families, nations, towns.   If
a certain number of clans are struggling for existence,
that portion of the conscience will be developed which
tends to the preservation of the clan; so, if towns or
families are struggling, we shall get a moral sense adapted
to the advantage of the town or the family.   In this
way different portions of the moral sense may be developed at different stages of progress.   Now it is clear
that for the purpose of the conscience the word " community " at any time will mean a group of that size and
nature which is being selected or not selected for survival
as a whole.   Selection may be going on at the same time
among many different kinds of groups.   And ultimately the moral sense will be composed of various
portions relating to various groups, the function or
purpose of each portion being the advantage of that
group to which it relates in the struggle for existence.
Thus we have a sense of family duty, of municipal duty,
of national duty, and of duties towards all mankind.

It is to be noticed that part of the nature of a smaller
group may be what it is for the sake of a larger group to
which it belongs; and then we may speak of the *function*
of the smaller group.   Thus it appears probable that the
family, in the form in which it now exists among us, is
determined by the good of the nation; and we may say
that the function of the family is to promote the advantage of the nation or larger society in some certain ways.
But I do not think it would be right to follow Auguste
Comte in speaking of the function of humanity; because
humanity is obviously not a part of any larger organism
for whose sake it is what it is.

Now that we have cleared up the meanings of some of our words, we are still a great way from the definite solution of our question, " What is the best conscience? or what ought I to think right? "   For we do not yet know what is for the advantage of the community in the struggle for existence.   If we choose to learn by the analogy of an individual organism, we may see that no permanent or final answer can be given, because the organism grows in consequence of the struggle, and develops new wants while it is satisfying the old ones. But at any given time it has quite enough to do to keep alive and to avoid dangers and diseases.   So we may expect that the wants and even the necessities of the social organism will grow with its growth, and that it is impossible to predict what may tend in the distant future to its advantage in the struggle for existence.   But still, in this vague and general statement of the functions of conscience, we shall find that we have already established a great deal.

In the first place, right is an affair of the community, and must not be referred to anything else.   To go back to our analogy of taste: if I tried to persuade you that the best palate was that which preferred things pretty to look at, you might condemn me *a priori*, without any experience, by merely knowing that taste is an affair of stomach and digestion—that its function is to select wholesome food.   And so, if anyone tries to persuade us that the best conscience is that which thinks it right to obey the will of some individual, as a deity or a monarch, he is condemned *a priori* in the very nature of right and wrong.   In order that the worship of a deity may be consistent with natural ethics, he must be regarded as the friend and helper of humanity, and his character must be judged from his actions by a moral standard which is independent of him.   And this, it must be admitted, is the position which has been taken by most English divines, as long as they were Englishmen first and divines afterwards.   The worship of a deity who is represented as unfair or unfriendly to any portion of the community is a wrong thing, however great may be the threats and promises by which it is commended. And still worse, the reference of right and wrong to his arbitrary will as a standard, the diversion of the allegiance of the moral sense from the community to him, is the most insidious and fatal of social diseases. It was against this that the Teutonic conscience protested in the Reformation. Again, in monarchical countries, in order that allegiance to the sovereign may be consistent with natural ethics, he must be regarded as the servant and symbol of the national unity, capable of rebellion and punishable for it. And this has been the theory of the English constitution from time immemorial.[1]

The first principle of natural ethics, then, is the sole and supreme allegiance of conscience to the community. I venture to call this *piety* in accordance with the older meaning of the word. Even if it should turn out impossible to sever it from the unfortunate associations which have clung to its later meaning, still it seems worth while to try.

An immediate deduction from our principle is that there are no self-regarding virtues properly so called; those qualities which tend to the advantage and preservation of the individual being only morally *right* in so far as they make him a more useful citizen. And this conclusion is in some cases of great practical importance. The virtue of purity, for example, attains in this way a fairly exact definition; purity in a man is that course of conduct which makes him to be a good husband and father, in a woman that which makes her to be a good wife and mother, or which helps other people so to prepare and keep themselves. It is easy to see how many false ideas and pernicious precepts are swept away by even so simple a definition as that.

Next, we may fairly define our position in regard to that moral system which has deservedly found favour with the great mass of our countrymen. In the common

---

[1] [Rex autem habet superiorem, Deum scilicet. Item legem per quam factus est rex. Item curiam suam . . . et ideo si rex fuerit sine fraeno, id est sine lege, debent ei fraenum ponere.—Bracton, fo. 34 *a*.]

statement of utilitarianism the end of right action is defined to be the greatest happiness of the greatest number. It seems to me that the reason and the ample justification of the success of this system is that it explicitly sets forth the community as the object of moral allegiance. But our determination of the purpose of the conscience will oblige us to make a change in the statement of it. Happiness is not the end of right action. My happiness is of no use to the community except in so far as it makes me a more efficient citizen; that is to say, it is rightly desired as a means and not as an end. The end may be described as the greatest efficiency of all citizens as such. No doubt happiness will in the long run accrue to the community as a consequence of right conduct; but the right is determined independently of the happiness, and, as Plato says, it is better to suffer wrong than to do wrong.

In conclusion, I would add some words on the relation of Veracity to the first principle of Piety. It is clear that veracity is founded on faith in man; you tell a man the truth when you can trust him with it and are not afraid. This perhaps is made more evident by considering the case of exception allowed by all moralists—namely, that if a man asks you the way with a view to committing a murder it is right to tell a lie and misdirect him. The reason why he must not have the truth told him is that he would make a bad use of it; he cannot be trusted with it. About these cases of exception an important remark must be made in passing. When we hear that a man has told a lie under such circumstances, we are indeed ready to admit that for once it was right, *mensonge admirable*; but we always have a sort of feeling that it must not occur again. And the same thing applies to cases of conflicting obligations, when for example the family conscience and the national conscience disagree. In such cases no general rule can be laid down; we have to choose the less of two evils; but this is not right altogether in the same sense as it is right to speak the truth. There is something wrong in the circumstances that we should have to choose an evil at all. The actual course to be pursued will vary with the progress of society; that evil which at first was greater will become less, and in a perfect society the conflict will be resolved into harmony. But meanwhile these cases of exception must be carefully kept distinct from the straightforward cases of right and wrong, and they always imply an obligation to mend the circumstances if we can.

Veracity to an individual is not only enjoined by piety in virtue of the obvious advantage which attends a straightforward and mutually trusting community as compared with others, but also because deception is in all cases a personal injury. Still more is this true of veracity to the community itself. The conception of the universe or aggregate of beliefs which forms the link between sensation and action for each individual is a public and not a private matter; it is formed by society and for society. Of what enormous importance it is to the community that this should be a true conception I need not attempt to describe. Now to the attainment of this true conception two things are necessary.

First, if we study the history of those methods by which true beliefs and false beliefs have been attained, we shall see that it is our duty to guide our beliefs by inference from experience on the assumption of uniformity of nature and consciousness in other men, *and by this only*. Only upon this moral basis can the foundations of the empirical method be justified.

Secondly, veracity to the community depends upon faith in man. Surely I ought to be talking platitudes when I say that it is not English to tell a man a lie, or to suggest a lie by your silence or your actions, because you are afraid that he is not prepared for the truth, because you don't quite know what he will do when he knows it, because perhaps after all this lie is a better thing for him than the truth would be, this same man being all the time an honest fellow-citizen whom you have every reason to trust. Surely I have heard that this craven crookedness is the object of our national detestation. And yet it is constantly whispered that it would be dangerous to divulge certain truths to the masses. " I know the whole thing is untrue: but then it is so useful for the people; you don't know what harm you might do by shaking their faith in it." Crooked ways are none the less crooked because they are meant to deceive great masses of people instead of individuals. If a thing is true let us all believe it, rich and poor, men, women, and children. If a thing is untrue let us all disbelieve it, rich and poor, men, women, and children. Truth is a thing to be shouted from the house-tops, not to be whispered over rose-water after dinner when the ladies are gone away.

Even in those whom I would most reverence, who would shrink with horror from such actual deception as I have just mentioned, I find traces of a want of faith in man. Even that noble thinker, to whom we of this generation owe more than I can tell, seemed to say in one of his posthumous essays that in regard to questions of great public importance we might encourage a hope in excess of the evidence (which would infallibly grow into a belief and defy evidence) if we found that life was made easier by it. As if we should not lose infinitely more by nourishing a tendency to falsehood than we could gain by the delusion of a pleasing fancy. Life must first of all be made straight and true; it may get easier through the help this brings to the commonwealth. And the great historian of materialism [1] says that the amount of false belief necessary to morality in a given society is a matter of taste. I cannot believe that any falsehood whatever is necessary to morality. It cannot be true of my race and yours that to keep ourselves from becoming scoundrels we must needs believe a lie. The sense of right grew up among healthy men and was fixed by the practice of comradeship. It has never had help from phantoms and falsehoods, and it never can want any. By faith in man and piety towards men we have taught each other the right hitherto; with faith in man and piety towards men we shall never more depart from it.

[1] Lange, *Geschichte des Materialismus.*

THE ETHICS OF BELIEF [1]

I.—THE DUTY OF INQUIRY

A SHIPOWNER was about to send to sea an emigrant ship. He knew that she was old, and not over-well built at the first; that she had seen many seas and climes, and often had needed repairs. Doubts had been suggested to him that possibly she was not seaworthy. These doubts preyed upon his mind and made him unhappy; he thought that perhaps he ought to have her thoroughly overhauled and refitted, even though this should put him to great expense. Before the ship sailed, however, he succeeded in overcoming these melancholy reflections. He said to himself that she had gone safely through so many voyages and weathered so many storms that it was idle to suppose she would not come safely home from this trip also. He would put his trust in Providence, which could hardly fail to protect all these unhappy families that were leaving their fatherland to seek for better times elsewhere. He would dismiss from his mind all ungenerous suspicions about the honesty of builders and contractors. In such ways he acquired a sincere and comfortable conviction that his vessel was thoroughly safe and seaworthy; he watched her departure with a light heart, and benevolent wishes for the success of the exiles in their strange new home that was to be; and he got his insurance-money when she went down in mid-ocean and told no tales.

What shall we say of him? Surely this, that he was verily guilty of the death of those men. It is admitted that he did sincerely believe in the soundness of his ship; but the sincerity of his conviction can in no wise help him, because *he had no right to believe on such evidence as was before him.* He had acquired his belief not by honestly earning it in patient investigation, but by stifling his doubts. And although in the end he may have felt so

[1] *Contemporary Review*, January, 1877.

sure about it that he could not think otherwise, yet inasmuch as he had knowingly and willingly worked himself into that frame of mind, he must be held responsible for it.

Let us alter the case a little, and suppose that the ship was not unsound after all; that she made her voyage safely, and many others after it. Will that diminish the guilt of her owner? Not one jot. When an action is once done, it is right or wrong for ever; no accidental failure of its good or evil fruits can possibly alter that. The man would not have been innocent, he would only have been not found out. The question of right or wrong has to do with the origin of his belief, not the matter of it; not what it was, but how he got it; not whether it turned out to be true or false, but whether he had a right to believe on such evidence as was before him.

There was once an island in which some of the inhabitants professed a religion teaching neither the doctrine of original sin nor that of eternal punishment. A suspicion got abroad that the professors of this religion had made use of unfair means to get their doctrines taught to children. They were accused of wresting the laws of their country in such a way as to remove children from the care of their natural and legal guardians; and even of stealing them away and keeping them concealed from their friends and relations. A certain number of men formed themselves into a society for the purpose of agitating the public about this matter. They published grave accusations against individual citizens of the highest position and character, and did all in their power to injure these citizens in the exercise of their professions. So great was the noise they made, that a Commission was appointed to investigate the facts; but after the Commission had carefully inquired into all the evidence that could be got, it appeared that the accused were innocent. Not only had they been accused on insufficient evidence, but the evidence of their innocence was such as the agitators might easily have obtained, if they had attempted a fair inquiry. After these disclosures the inhabitants of that country looked upon the members of the agitating society, not only as persons whose judgment was to be distrusted, but also as no longer to be counted honourable men. For although they had sincerely and conscientiously believed in the charges they had made, *yet they had no right to believe on such evidence as was before them.* Their sincere convictions, instead of being honestly earned by patient inquiring, were stolen by listening to the voice of prejudice and passion.

Let us vary this case also, and suppose, other things remaining as before, that a still more accurate investigation proved the accused to have been really guilty. Would this make any difference in the guilt of the accusers? Clearly not; the question is not whether their belief was true or false, but whether they entertained it on wrong grounds. They would no doubt say: " Now you see that we were right after all; next time perhaps you will believe us." And they might be believed, but they would not thereby become honourable men. They would not be innocent, they would only be not found out. Every one of them, if he chose to examine himself *in foro conscientiæ*, would know that he had acquired and nourished a belief, when he had no right to believe on such evidence as was before him; and therein he would know that he had done a wrong thing.

It may be said, however, that in both of these supposed cases it is not the belief which is judged to be wrong, but the action following upon it. The shipowner might say: " I am perfectly certain that my ship is sound, but still I feel it my duty to have her examined, before trusting the lives of so many people to her." And it might be said to the agitator: " However convinced you were of the justice of your cause and the truth of your convictions, you ought not to have made a public attack upon any man's character until you had examined the evidence on both sides with the utmost patience and care."

In the first place, let us admit that, so far as it goes, this view of the case is right and necessary; right, because even when a man's belief is so fixed that he cannot think otherwise, he still has a choice in regard to the action suggested by it, and so cannot escape the duty of investigating on the ground of the strength of his convictions; and necessary, because those who are not yet capable of controlling their feelings and thoughts must have a plain rule dealing with overt acts.

But this being premised as necessary, it becomes clear that it is not sufficient, and that our previous judgment is required to supplement it. For it is not possible so to sever the belief from the action it suggests as to condemn the one without condemning the other. No man holding a strong belief on one side of a question, or even wishing to hold a belief on one side, can investigate it with such fairness and completeness as if he were really in doubt and unbiased; so that the existence of a belief not founded on fair inquiry unfits a man for the performance of this necessary duty.

Nor. is that truly a belief at all which has not some influence upon the actions of him who holds it. He who truly believes that which prompts him to an action has looked upon the action to lust after it, he has committed it already in his heart. If a belief is not realised immediately in open deeds, it is stored up for the guidance of the future. It goes to make a part of that aggregate of beliefs which is the link between sensation and action at every moment of all our lives, and which is so organised and compacted together that no part of it can be isolated from the rest, but every new addition modifies the structure of the whole. No real belief, however trifling and fragmentary it may seem, is ever truly insignificant; it prepares us to receive more of its like, confirms those which resembled it before, and weakens others; and so gradually it lays a stealthy train in our inmost thoughts, which may some day explode into overt action, and leave its stamp upon our character for ever.

And no one man's belief is in any case a private matter which concerns himself alone. Our lives are guided by that general conception of the course of things which has been created by society for social purposes. Our words, our phrases, our forms and processes and modes of thought, are common property, fashioned and perfected from age to age; an heirloom which every succeeding generation inherits as a precious deposit and a sacred trust to be handed on to the next one, not unchanged but enlarged and purified, with some clear marks of its proper handiwork. Into this, for good or ill, is woven every belief of every man who has speech of his fellows. An awful privilege, and an awful responsibility, that we should help to create the world in which posterity will live.

In the two supposed cases which have been considered, it has been judged wrong to believe on insufficient evidence, or to nourish belief by suppressing doubts and avoiding investigation. The reason of this judgment is not far to seek: it is that in both these cases the belief held by one man was of great importance to other men. But forasmuch as no belief held by one man, however seemingly trivial the belief, and however obscure the believer, is ever actually insignificant or without its effect on the fate of mankind, we have no choice but to extend our judgment to all .cases of belief whatever. Belief, that sacred faculty which prompts the decisions of our will, and knits into harmonious working all the compacted energies of our being, is ours not for ourselves, but for humanity. It is rightly used on truths which have been established by long experience and waiting toil, and which have stood in the fierce light of free and fearless questioning. Then it helps to bind men together, and to strengthen and direct their common action. It is desecrated when given to unproved and unquestioned statements, for the solace and private pleasure of the believer; to add a tinsel splendour to the plain straight road of our life and display a bright mirage beyond it; or even to drown the common sorrows of our kind by a self-deception which allows them not only to cast down, but also to degrade us. Whoso would deserve well of his fellows in this matter will guard the purity of his belief with a very fanaticism of jealous care, lest at any time it should rest on an unworthy object, and catch a stain which can never be wiped away.

It is not only the leader of men, statesman, philosopher, or poet, that owes this bounden duty to mankind. Every rustic who delivers in the village alehouse his slow, infrequent sentences, may help to kill or keep alive the fatal superstitions which clog his race. Every hard-worked wife of an artisan may transmit to her children beliefs which shall knit society together, or rend it in pieces. No simplicity of mind, no obscurity of station, can escape the universal duty of questioning all that we believe.

It is true that this duty is a hard one, and the doubt which comes out of it is often a very bitter thing. It leaves us bare and powerless where we thought that we were safe and strong. To know all about anything is to know how to deal with it under all circumstances. We feel much happier and more secure when we think we know precisely what to do, no matter what happens, than when we have lost our way and do not know where to turn. And if we have supposed ourselves to know all about anything, and to be capable of doing what is fit in regard to it, we naturally do not like to find that we are really ignorant and powerless, that we have to begin again at the beginning, and try to learn what the thing is and how it is to be dealt with—if indeed anything can be learnt about it. It is the sense of power attached to a sense of knowledge that makes men desirous of believing, and afraid of doubting.

This sense of power is the highest and best of pleasures when the belief on which it is founded is a true belief, and has been fairly earned by investigation. For then we may justly feel that it is common property, and holds good for others as well as for ourselves. Then we may be glad, not that *I* have learned secrets by which I am safer and stronger, but that *we men* have got mastery over more of the world; and we shall be strong, not for ourselves, but in the name of Man and in his strength. But if the belief has been accepted on insufficient evidence, the pleasure is a stolen one. Not only does it deceive ourselves by giving us a sense of power which we do not really possess, but it is sinful, because it is stolen in defiance of our duty to mankind. That duty is to guard ourselves from such beliefs as from a pestilence, which may shortly master our own body and then spread to the rest of the town. What would be thought of one who, for the sake of a sweet fruit, should deliberately run the risk of bringing a plague upon his family and his neighbours?

And, as in other such cases, it is not the risk only which has to be considered; for a bad action is always bad at the time when it is done, no matter what happens afterwards. Every time we let ourselves believe for unworthy reasons, we weaken our powers of self-control, of doubting, of judicially and fairly weighing evidence. We all suffer severely enough from the maintenance and support of false beliefs and the fatally wrong actions which they lead to, and the evil born when one such belief is entertained is great and wide. But a greater and wider evil arises when the credulous character is maintained and supported, when a habit of believing for unworthy reasons is fostered and made permanent. If I steal money from any person, there may be no harm done by the mere transfer of possession; he may not feel the loss, or it may prevent him from using the money badly. But I cannot help doing this great wrong towards Man, that I make myself dishonest. What hurts society is not that it should lose its property, but that it should become a den of thieves; for then it must cease to be society. This is why we ought not to do evil that good may come; for at any rate this great evil has come, that we have done evil and are made wicked thereby. In like manner, if I let myself believe anything on insufficient evidence, there may be no great harm done by the mere belief; it may be true after all, or I may never have occasion to exhibit it in outward acts. But I cannot help doing this great wrong towards Man, that I make myself credulous. The danger to society is not merely that it should believe wrong things, though that is great enough; but that it should become credulous, and lose the habit of testing things and inquiring into them; for then it must sink back into savagery.

The harm which is done by credulity in a man is not confined to the fostering of a credulous character in others, and consequent support of false beliefs. Habitual want of care about what I believe leads to habitual want of care in others about the truth of what is told to me. Men speak the truth to one another when each reveres the truth in his own mind and in the other's mind; but how shall my friend revere the truth in my mind when I myself am careless about it, when I believe things because I want to believe them, and because they are comforting and pleasant? Will he not learn to cry, " Peace," to me, when there is no peace? By such a course I shall surround myself with a thick atmosphre of falsehood and fraud, and in that I must live. It may matter little to me, in my cloud-castle of sweet illusions and darling lies; but it matters much to Man that I have made my neighbours ready to deceive. The credulous man is father to the liar and the cheat; he lives in the bosom of this his family, and it is no marvel if he should become even as they are. So closely are our duties knit together, that whoso shall keep the whole law, and yet offend in one point, he is guilty of all.

To sum up; it is wrong always, everywhere, and for anyone, to believe anything upon insufficient evidence.

If a man, holding a belief which he was taught in childhood or persuaded of afterwards, keeps down and pushes away any doubts which arise about it in his mind, purposely avoids the reading of books and the company of men that call in question or discuss it, and regards as impious those questions which cannot easily be asked without disturbing it—the life of that man is one long sin against mankind.

If this judgment seems harsh when applied to those simple souls who have never known better, who have been brought up from the cradle with a horror of doubt, and taught that their eternal welfare depends on *what* they believe, then it leads to the very serious question, *Who hath made Israel to sin?*

It may be permitted me to fortify this judgment with the sentence of Milton [1]—

" A man may be a heretic in the truth; and if he

[1] *Areopagitica.*

believe things only because his pastor says so, or the assembly so determine, without knowing other reason, though his belief be true, yet the very truth he holds becomes his heresy."

And with this famous aphorism of Coleridge [1] :—

" He who begins by loving Christianity better than Truth, will proceed by loving his own sect or Church better than Christianity, and end in loving himself better than all."

Inquiry into the evidence of a doctrine is not to be made once for all, and then taken as finally settled. It is never lawful to stifle a doubt; for either it can be honestly answered by means of the inquiry already made, or else it proves that the inquiry was not complete.

" But," says one, " I am a busy man; I have no time for the long course of study which would be necessary to make me in any degree a competent judge of certain questions, or even able to understand the nature of the arguments." Then he should have no time to believe.

II.—THE WEIGHT OF AUTHORITY

Are we then to become universal sceptics, doubting everything, afraid always to put one foot before the other until we have personally tested the firmness of the road? Are we to deprive ourselves of the help and guidance of that vast body of knowledge which is daily growing upon the world, because neither we nor any other one person can possibly test a hundredth part of it by immediate experiment or observation, and because it would not be completely proved if we did? Shall we steal and tell lies because we have had no personal experience wide enough to justify the belief that it is wrong to do so?

There is no practical danger that such consequences will ever follow from scrupulous care and self-control in the matter of belief. Those men who have most nearly done their duty in this respect have found that certain

[1] *Aids to Reflection.*

great principles, and these most fitted for the guidance of life, have stood out more and more clearly in proportion to the care and honesty with which they were tested, and have acquired in this way a practical certainty. The beliefs about right and wrong which guide our actions in dealing with men in society, and the beliefs about physical nature which guide our actions in dealing with animate and inanimate bodies, these never suffer from investigation; they can take care of themselves, without being propped up by " acts of faith," the clamour of paid advocates, or the suppression of contrary evidence. Moreover there are many cases in which it is our duty to act upon probabilities, although the evidence is not such as to justify present belief; because it is precisely by such action, and by observation of its fruits, that evidence is got which may justify future belief. So that we have no reason to fear lest a habit of conscientious inquiry should paralyse the actions of our daily life.

But because it is not enough to say, " It is wrong to believe on unworthy evidence," without saying also what evidence is worthy, we shall now go on to inquire under what circumstances it is lawful to believe on the testimony of others; and then, further, we shall inquire more generally when and why we may believe that which goes beyond our own experience, or even beyond the experience of mankind.

In what cases, then, let us ask in the first place, is the testimony of a man unworthy of belief? He may say that which is untrue either knowingly or unknowingly. In the first case he is lying, and his moral character is to blame; in the second case he is ignorant or mistaken, and it is only his knowledge or his judgment which is in fault. In order that we may have the right to accept his testimony as ground for believing what he says, we must have reasonable grounds for trusting his *veracity*, that he is really trying to speak the truth so far as he knows it; his *knowledge*, that he has had opportunities of knowing the truth about this matter; and his *judgment*, that he has made proper use of those opportunities in coming to the conclusion which he affirms.

However plain and obvious these reasons may be, so that no man of ordinary intelligence, reflecting upon the matter, could fail to arrive at them, it is nevertheless true that a great many persons do habitually disregard them in weighing testimony. Of the two questions, equally important to the trustworthiness of a witness, " Is he dishonest? " and " May he be mistaken? " the majority of mankind are perfectly satisfied if *one* can, with some show of probability, be answered in the negative. The excellent moral character of a man is alleged as ground for accepting his statements about things which he cannot possibly have known. A Mohammedan, for example, will tell us that the character of his Prophet was so noble and majestic that it commands the reverence even of those who do not believe in his mission. So admirable was his moral teaching, so wisely put together the great social machine which he created, that his precepts have not only been accepted by a great portion of mankind, but have actually been obeyed. His institutions have on the one hand rescued the negro from savagery, and on the other hand have taught civilisation to the advancing West; and although the races which held the highest forms of his faith, and most fully embodied his mind and thought, have all been conquered and swept away by barbaric tribes, yet the history of their marvellous attainments remains as an imperishable glory to Islam. Are we to doubt the word of a man so great and so good? Can we suppose that this magnificent genius, this splendid moral hero, has lied to us about the most solemn and sacred matters? The testimony of Mohammed is clear, that there is but one God, and that he, Mohammed, is his Prophet; that if we believe in him we shall enjoy everlasting felicity, but that if we do not we shall be damned. This testimony rests on the most awful of foundations, the revelation of heaven itself; for was he not visited by the angel Gabriel, as he fasted and prayed in his desert cave, and allowed to enter into the blessed fields of Paradise? Surely God is God and Mohammed is the Prophet of God.

What should we answer to this Mussulman? First,

no doubt, we should be tempted to take exception against his view of the character of the Prophet and the uniformly beneficial influence of Islam: before we could go with him altogether in these matters it might seem that we should have to forget many terrible things of which we have heard or read. But if we chose to grant him all these assumptions, for the sake of argument, and because it is difficult both for the faithful and for infidels to discuss them fairly and without passion, still we should have something to say which takes away the ground of his belief, and therefore shows that it is wrong to entertain it. Namely this: the character of Mohammed is excellent evidence that he was honest and spoke the truth so far as he knew it; but it is no evidence at all that he knew what the truth was. What means could he have of knowing that the form which appeared to him to be the angel Gabriel was not a hallucination, and that his apparent visit to Paradise was not a dream? Grant that he himself was fully persuaded and honestly believed that he had the guidance of heaven, and was the vehicle of a supernatural revelation, how could he know that this strong conviction was not a mistake? Let us put ourselves in his place; we shall find that the more completely we endeavour to realise what passed through his mind, the more clearly we shall perceive that the Prophet could have had no adequate ground for the belief in his own inspiration. It is most probable that he himself never doubted of the matter, or thought of asking the question; but we are in the position of those to whom the question has been asked, and who are bound to answer it. It is known to medical observers that solitude and want of food are powerful means of producing delusion and of fostering a tendency to mental disease. Let us suppose, then, that I, like Mohammed, go into desert places to fast and pray; what things can happen to me which will give me the right to believe that I am divinely inspired? Suppose that I get information, apparently from a celestial visitor, which upon being tested is found to be correct. I cannot be sure, in the first place, that the celestial visitor is not a figment of my own mind, and that the information did not come to me, unknown at the time to my consciousness, through some subtle channel of sense. But if my visitor was a real visitor, and for a long time gave me information which was found to be trustworthy, this would indeed be good ground for trusting him in the future as to such matters as fall within human powers of verification; but it would not be ground for trusting his testimony as to any other matters. For although his tested character would justify me in believing that he spoke the truth so far as he knew, yet the same question would present itself: What ground is there for supposing that he knows?

Even if my supposed visitor had given me such information, subsequently verified by me, as proved him to have means of knowledge about verifiable matters far exceeding my own; this would not justify me in believing what he said about matters that are not at present capable of verification by man. It would be ground for interesting conjecture, and for the hope that, as the fruit of our patient inquiry, we might by and by attain to such a means of verification as should rightly turn conjecture into belief. For belief belongs to man, and to the guidance of human affairs: no belief is real unless it guide our actions, and those very actions supply a test of its truth.

But, it may be replied, the acceptance of Islam as a system is just that action which is prompted by belief in the mission of the Prophet, and which will serve for a test of its truth. Is it possible to believe that a system which has succeeded so well is really founded upon a delusion? Not only have individual saints found joy and peace in believing, and verified those spiritual experiences which are promised to the faithful, but nations also have been raised from savagery or barbarism to a higher social state. Surely we are at liberty to say that the belief has been acted upon, and that it has been verified.

It requires, however, but little consideration to show that what has really been verified is not at all the supernal character of the Prophet's mission, or the trustworthiness of his authority in matters which we ourselves cannot test, but only his practical wisdom in certain very mundane things. The fact that believers have found joy and peace in believing gives us the right to say that the doctrine is a comfortable doctrine, and pleasant to the soul; but it does not give us the right to say that it is true. And the question which our conscience is always asking about that which we are tempted to believe is not, " Is it comfortable and pleasant? " but, " Is it true? " That the Prophet preached certain doctrines, and predicted that spiritual comfort would be found in them, proves only his sympathy with human nature and his knowledge of it; but it does not prove his superhuman knowledge of theology.

And if we admit for the sake of argument (for it seems that we cannot do more) that the progress made by Moslem nations in certain cases was really due to the system formed and sent forth into the world by Mohammed, we are not at liberty to conclude from this that he was inspired to declare the truth about things which we cannot verify. We are only at liberty to infer the excellence of his moral precepts, or of the means which he devised for so working upon men so as to get them obeyed, or of the social and political machinery which he set up. And it would require a great amount of careful examination into the history of those nations to determine which of these things had the greater share in the result. So that here again it is the Prophet's knowledge of human nature, and his sympathy with it, that are verified; not his divine inspiration or his knowledge of theology.

If there were only one Prophet, indeed, it might well seem a difficult and even an ungracious task to decide upon what points we would trust him, and on what we would doubt his authority; seeing what help and furtherance all men have gained in all ages from those who saw more clearly, who felt more strongly, and who sought the truth with more single heart than their weaker brethren. But there is not only one Prophet; and while the consent of many upon that which, as men, they had real means of knowing and did know, has endured to the end, and been honourably built into the great fabric of human knowledge, the diverse witness of some about that which they did not and could not know remains as a warning to us that to exaggerate the prophetic authority is to misuse it, and to dishonour those who have sought only to help and further us after their power. It is hardly in human nature that a man should quite accurately gauge the limits of his own insight; but it is the duty of those who profit by his work to consider carefully where he may have been carried beyond it. If we must needs embalm his possible errors along with his solid achievements, and use his authority as an excuse for believing what he cannot have known, we make of his goodness an occasion to sin.

To consider only one other such witness: the followers of the Buddha have at least as much right to appeal to individual and social experience in support of the authority of the Eastern saviour. The special mark of his religion, it is said, that in which it has never been surpassed, is the comfort and consolation which it gives to the sick and sorrowful, the tender sympathy with which it soothes and assuages all the natural griefs of men. And surely no triumph of social morality can be greater or nobler than that which has kept nearly half the human race from persecuting in the name of religion. If we are to trust the accounts of his early followers, he believed himself to have come upon earth with a divine and cosmic mission to set rolling the wheel of the law. Being a prince, he divested himself of his kingdom, and of his free will became acquainted with misery, that he might learn how to meet and subdue it. Could such a man speak falsely about solemn things? And as for his knowledge, was he not a man miraculous with powers more than man's? He was born of woman without the help of man; he rose into the air and was transfigured before his kinsmen; at last he went up bodily into heaven from the top of Adam's Peak. Is not his word to be believed in when he testifies of heavenly things?

If there were only he, and no other, with such claims! But there is Mohammed with his testimony; we cannot

choose but listen to them both. The Prophet tells us
that there is one God, and that we shall live for ever in
joy or misery, according as we believe in the Prophet or
not. The Buddha says that there is no God, and that
we shall be annihilated by and by if we are good enough.
Both cannot be infallibly inspired; one or other must
have been the victim of a delusion, and thought he knew
that which he really did not know. Who shall dare to
say which? and how can we justify ourselves in believing
that the other was not also deluded?

We are led, then, to these judgments following. The
goodness and greatness of a man do not justify us in
accepting a belief upon the warrant of his authority,
unless there are reasonable grounds for supposing that
he knew the truth of what he was saying. And there can
be no grounds for supposing that a man knows that which
we, without ceasing to be men, could not be supposed to
verify.

If a chemist tells me, who am no chemist, that a
certain substance can be made by putting together other
substances in certain proportions and subjecting them to
a known process, I am quite justified in believing this
upon his authority, unless I know anything against his
character or his judgment. For his professional training
is one which tends to encourage veracity and the honest
pursuit of truth, and to produce a dislike of hasty conclusions and slovenly investigation. And I have reasonable ground for supposing that he knows the truth of
what he is saying, for although I am no chemist, I can
be made to understand so much of the methods and
processes of the science as makes it conceivable to me
that, without ceasing to be man, I might verify the
statement. I may never actually verify it, or even see
any experiment which goes towards verifying it; but still
I have quite reason enough to justify me in believing
that the verification is within the reach of human appliances and powers, and in particular that it has been
actually performed by my informant. His result, the
belief to which he has been led by his inquiries, is valid
not only for himself but for others; it is watched and

tested by those who are working in the same ground, and who know that no greater service can be rendered to science than the purification of accepted results from the errors which may have crept into them. It is in this way that the result becomes common property, a right object of belief, which is a social affair and matter of public business. Thus it is to be observed that his authority is valid because there are those who question it and verify it; that it is precisely this process of examining and purifying that keeps alive among investigators the love of that which shall stand all possible tests, the sense of public responsibility as of those whose work, if well done, shall remain as the enduring heritage of mankind.

But if my chemist tells me that an atom of oxygen has existed unaltered in weight and rate of vibration throughout all time, I have no right to believe this on his authority, for it is a thing which he cannot know without ceasing to be man. He may quite honestly believe that this statement is a fair inference from his experiments, but in that case his judgment is at fault. A very simple consideration of the character of experiments would show him that they never can lead to results of such a kind; that, being themselves only approximate and limited, they cannot give us knowledge which is exact and universal. No eminence of character and genius can give a man authority enough to justify us in believing him when he makes statements implying exact or universal knowledge.

Again, an arctic explorer may tell us that in a given latitude and longitude he has experienced such and such a degree of cold, that the sea was of such a depth, and the ice of such a character. We should be quite right to believe him, in the absence of any stain upon his veracity. It is conceivable that we might, without ceasing to be men, go there and verify his statement; it can be tested by the witness of his companions, and there is adequate ground for supposing that he knows the truth of what he is saying. But if an old whaler tells us that the ice is 300 feet thick all the way up to the Pole, we shall not be justified in believing him. For although the statement may be capable of verification by man, it is certainly not capable of verification by *him*, with any means and appliances which he has possessed; and he must have persuaded himself of the truth of it by some means which does not attach any credit to his testimony. Even if, therefore, the matter affirmed is within the reach of human knowledge, we have no right to accept it upon authority unless it is within the reach of our informant's knowledge.

What shall we say of that authority, more venerable and august than any individual witness, the time-honoured tradition of the human race? An atmosphere of beliefs and conceptions has been formed by the labours and struggles of our forefathers, which enables us to breathe amid the various and complex circumstances of our life. It is around and about us and within us; we cannot think except in the forms and processes of thought which it supplies. Is it possible to doubt and to test it? and if possible, is it right?

We shall find reason to answer that it is not only possible and right, but our bounden duty; that the main purpose of the tradition itself is to supply us with the means of asking questions, of testing and inquiring into things; that if we misuse it, and take it as a collection of cut-and-dried statements to be accepted without further inquiry, we are not only injuring ourselves here, but, by refusing to do our part towards the building up of the fabric which shall be inherited by our children, we are tending to cut off ourselves and our race from the human line.

Let us first take care to distinguish a kind of tradition which especially requires to be examined and called in question, because it especially shrinks from inquiry. Suppose that a medicine-man in Central Africa tells his tribe that a certain powerful medicine in his tent will be propitiated if they kill their catttle, and that the tribe believe him. Whether the medicine was propitiated or not there are no means of verifying, but the cattle are gone. Still the belief may be kept up in the tribe that propitiation has been effected in this way; and in a later generation it will be all the easier for another medicine-man to persuade them to a similar act. Here the only reason for belief is that everybody has believed the thing for so long that it must be true. And yet the belief was founded on fraud and has been propagated by credulity. That man will undoubtedly do right, and be a friend of men, who shall call it in question and see that there is no evidence for it, help his neighbours to see as he does, and even, if need be, go into the holy tent and break the medicine.

The rule which should guide us in such cases is simple and obvious enough: that the aggregate testimony of our neighbours is subject to the same conditions as the testimony of any one of them. Namely, we have no right to believe a thing true because everybody says so unless there are good grounds for believing that some one person at least has the means of knowing what is true, and is speaking the truth so far as he knows it. However many nations and generations of men are brought into the witness-box, they cannot testify to anything which they do not know. Every man who has accepted the statement from somebody else, without himself testing and verifying it, is out of court; his word is worth nothing at all. And when we get back at last to the true birth and beginning of the statement, two serious questions must be disposed of in regard to him who first made it: was he mistaken in thinking that he *knew* about this matter, or was he lying?

This last question is unfortunately a very actual and practical one even to us at this day and in this country. We have no occasion to go to La Salette, or to Central Africa, or to Lourdes, for examples of immoral and debasing superstition. It is only too possible for a child to grow up in London surrounded by an atmosphere of beliefs fit only for the savage, which have in our own time been founded in fraud and propagated by credulity.

Laying aside, then, such tradition as is handed on without testing by successive generations, let us consider that which is truly built up out of the common experience of mankind. This great fabric is for the guidance of our thoughts, and through them of our actions, both in the moral and in the material world.   In the moral world, for example, it gives us the conceptions of right in general, of justice, of truth, of beneficence, and the like.   These are given as conceptions, not as statements or propositions; they answer to certain definite instincts which are certainly within us, however they came there.   That it is right to be beneficent is matter of immediate personal experience; for when a man retires within himself and there finds something, wider and more lasting than his solitary personality, which says, " I want to do right," as well as, " I want to do good to man," he can verify by direct observation that one instinct is founded upon and agrees fully with the other.   And it is his duty so to verify this and all similar statements.

The tradition says also, at a definite place and time, that such and such actions are just, or true, or beneficent. For all such rules a further inquiry is necessary, since they are sometimes established by an authority other than that of the moral sense founded on experience.   Until recently, the moral tradition of our own country—and indeed of all Europe—taught that it was beneficent to give money indiscriminately to beggars.   But the questioning of this rule, and investigation into it, led men to see that true beneficence is that which helps a man to do the work which he is most fitted for, not that which keeps and encourages him in idleness; and that to neglect this distinction in the present is to prepare pauperism and misery for the future.   By this testing and discussion not only has practice been purified and made more beneficent, but the very conception of beneficence has been made wider and wiser.   Now here the great social heirloom consists of two parts; the instinct of beneficence, which makes a certain side of our nature, when predominant, wish to do good to men; and the intellectual conception of beneficence, which we can compare with any proposed course of conduct and ask, " Is this beneficent or not? "   By the continual asking and answering of such questions the conception grows in breadth and distinctness, and the instinct becomes strengthened and purified.   It appears, then, that the great use of the conception, the intellectual part of the heirloom, is to enable us to ask questions; that it grows and is kept straight by means of these questions; and if we do not use it for that purpose we shall gradually lose it altogether, and be left with a mere code of regulations which cannot rightly be called morality at all.

Such considerations apply even more obviously and clearly, if possible, to the store of beliefs and conceptions which our fathers have amassed for us in respect of the material world. We are ready to laugh at the rule of thumb of the Australian who continues to tie his hatchet to the side of the handle, although the Birmingham fitter has made a hole on purpose for him to put the handle in. His people have tied up hatchets so for ages: who is he that he should set himself up against their wisdom? He has sunk so low that he cannot do what some of them must have done in the far distant past—call in question an established usage, and invent or learn something better. Yet here, in the dim beginning of knowledge, where science and art are one, we find only the same simple rule which applies to the highest and deepest growths of that cosmic Tree; to its loftiest flower-tipped branches as well as to the profoundest of its hidden roots; the rule, namely, that what is stored up and handed down to us is rightly used by those who act as the makers acted, when they stored it up; those who use it to ask further questions, to examine, to investigate; who try honestly and solemnly to find out what is the right way of looking at things and of dealing with them.

A question rightly asked is already half answered, said Jacobi; we may add that the method of solution is the other half of the answer, and that the actual result counts for nothing by the side of these two. For an example let us go to the telegraph, where theory and practice, grown each to years of discretion, are marvellously wedded for the fruitful service of men. Ohm found that the strength of an electric current is directly proportional to the strength of the battery which produces it, and inversely as the length of the wire along which it has to travel. This is called Ohm's law; but the result, regarded as a statement to be believed, is not the valuable part of it. The first half is the question: What relation holds good between these quantities? So put, the question involves already the conception of strength of current, and of strength of battery, as quantities to be measured and compared; it hints clearly that these are the things to be attended to in the study of electric currents. The second half is the method of investigation: how to measure these quantities, what instruments are required for the experiment, and how are they to be used? The student who begins to learn about electricity is not asked to believe in Ohm's law; he is made to understand the question, he is placed before the apparatus, and he is taught to verify it. He learns to do things, not to think he knows things; to use instruments and to ask questions, not to accept a traditional statement. The question which required a genius to ask it rightly is answered by a tiro. If Ohm's law were suddenly lost and forgotten by all men, while the question and the method of solution remained, the result could be rediscovered in an hour. But the result by itself, if known to a people who could not comprehend the value of the question or the means of solving it, would be like a watch in the hands of a savage who could not wind it up, or an iron steamship worked by Spanish engineers.

In regard, then, to the sacred tradition of humanity, we learn that it consists, not in propositions or statements which are to be accepted and believed on the authority of the tradition, but in questions rightly asked, in conceptions which enable us to ask further questions, and in methods of answering questions. The value of all these things depends on their being tested day by day. The very sacredness of the precious deposit imposes upon us the duty and the responsibility of testing it, of purifying and enlarging it to the utmost of our power. He who makes use of its results to stifle his own doubts, or to hamper the inquiry of others, is guilty of a sacrilege which centuries shall never be able to blot out. When the labours and questionings of honest and brave men shall have built up the fabric of known truth to a glory which we in this generation can neither hope for nor imagine, in that pure and holy temple he shall have no part nor lot, but his name and his works shall be cast out into the darkness of oblivion for ever.

III.—THE LIMITS OF INFERENCE

The question in what cases we may believe that which goes beyond our experience, is a very large and delicate one, extending to the whole range of scientific method, and requiring a considerable increase in the application of it before it can be answered with anything approaching to completeness. But one rule, lying on the threshold of the subject, of extreme simplicity and vast practical importance, may here be touched upon and shortly laid down.

A little reflection will show us that every belief, even the simplest and most fundamental, goes beyond experience when regarded as a guide to our actions. A burnt child dreads the fire, because it believes that the fire will burn it to-day just as it did yesterday; but this belief goes beyond experience, and assumes that the unknown fire of to-day is like the known fire of yesterday. Even the belief that the child was burnt yesterday goes beyond *present* experience, which contains only the memory of a burning, and not the burning itself; it assumes, therefore, that this memory is trustworthy, although we know that a memory may often be mistaken. But if it is to be used as a guide to action, as a hint of what the future is to be, it must assume something about that future, namely, that it will be consistent with the supposition that the burning really took place yesterday; which is going beyond experience. Even the fundamental " I am," which cannot be doubted, is no guide to action until it takes to itself " I shall be," which goes beyond experience. The question is not, therefore, " May we believe what goes beyond experience? " for this is involved in the very nature of belief; but " How far and in what manner may we add to our experience in forming our beliefs? "

And an answer, of utter simplicity and universality, is suggested by the example we have taken: a burnt child dreads the fire. We may go beyond experience by assuming that what we do not know is like what we do know; or, in other words, we may add to our experience on the assumption of a uniformity in nature. What this uniformity precisely is, how we grow in the knowledge of it from generation to generation, these are questions which for the present we lay aside, being content to examine two instances which may serve to make plainer the nature of the rule.

From certain observations made with the spectroscope, we infer the existence of hydrogen in the sun. By looking into the spectroscope when the sun is shining on its slit, we see certain definite bright lines: and experiments made upon bodies on the earth have taught us that when these bright lines are seen hydrogen is the source of them. We assume, then, that the unknown bright lines in the sun are like the known bright lines of the laboratory, and that hydrogen in the sun behaves as hydrogen under similar circumstances would behave on the earth.

But are we not trusting our spectroscope too much? Surely, having found it to be trustworthy for terrestrial substances, where its statements can be verified by man, we are justified in accepting its testimony in other like cases; but not when it gives us information about things in the sun, where its testimony cannot be directly verified by man?

Certainly, we want to know a little more before this inference can be justified; and fortunately we do know this. The spectroscope testifies to exactly the same thing in the two cases; namely, that light-vibrations of a certain rate are being sent through it. Its construction is such that if it were wrong about this in one case, it would be wrong in the other. When we come to look into the matter, we find that we have really assumed the matter of the sun to be like the matter of the earth, made up of a certain number of distinct substances; and that each of these, when very hot, has a distinct rate of vibration, by which it may be recognised and singled out from the rest.   But this is the kind of assumption which we are justified in using when we add to our experience.   It is an assumption of uniformity in nature, and can only be checked by comparison with many similar assumptions which we have to make in other such cases.

But is this a true belief, of the existence of hydrogen in the sun?   Can it help in the right guidance of human action?

Certainly not, if it is accepted on unworthy grounds, and without some understanding of the process by which it is got at.   But when this process is taken in as the ground of the belief, it becomes a very serious and practical matter.   For if there is no hydrogen in the sun, the spectroscope—that is to say, the measurement of rates of vibration—must be an uncertain guide in recognising different substances; and consequently it ought not to be used in chemical analysis—in assaying, for example—to the great saving of time, trouble, and money. Whereas the acceptance of the spectroscopic method as trustworthy has enriched us not only with new metals, which is a great thing, but with new processes of investigation, which is vastly greater.

For another example, let us consider the way in which we infer the truth of an historical event—say the siege of Syracuse in the Peloponnesian war.   Our experience is that manuscripts exist which are said to be and which call themselves manuscripts of the history of Thucydides; that in other manuscripts, stated to be by later historians, he is described as living during the time of the war; and that books, supposed to date from the revival of learning, tell us how these manuscripts had been preserved and were then acquired.   We find also that men do not, as a rule, forge books and histories without a special motive; we assume that in this respect men in the past were like men in the present; and we observe that in this case no special motive was present.   That is, we add to our experience on the assumption of a uniformity in the characters of men.   Because our knowledge of this uniformity is far less complete and exact than our knowledge of that which obtains in physics, inferences of the historical kind are more precarious and less exact than inferences in many other sciences.

But if there is any special reason to suspect the character of the persons who wrote or transmitted certain books, the case becomes altered. If a group of documents give internal evidence that they were produced among people who forged books in the names of others, and who, in describing events, suppressed those things which did not suit them, while they amplified such as did suit them; who not only committed these crimes, but gloried in them as proofs of humility and zeal; then we must say that upon such documents no true historical inference can be founded, but only unsatisfactory conjecture.

We may, then, add to our experience on the assumption of a uniformity in nature; we may fill in our picture of what is and has been, as experience gives it us, in such a way as to make the whole consistent with this uniformity. And practically demonstrative inference—that which gives us a right to believe in the result of it—is a clear showing that in no other way than by the truth of this result can the uniformity of nature be saved.

No evidence, therefore, can justify us in believing the truth of a statement which is contrary to, or outside of, the uniformity of nature. If our experience is such that it cannot be filled up consistently with uniformity, all we have a right to conclude is that there is something wrong somewhere; but the possibility of inference is taken away; we must rest in our experience, and not go beyond it at all. If an event really happened which was not a part of the uniformity of nature, it would have two properties: no evidence could give the right to believe it to any except those whose actual experience it was; and no inference worthy of belief could be founded upon it at all.

Are we then bound to believe that nature is absolutely and universally uniform? Certainly not, we have no right to believe anything of this kind. The rule only tells us that in forming beliefs which go beyond our experience we may make the assumption that nature is practically uniform so far as we are concerned. Within the range of human action and verification, we may form, by help of this assumption, actual beliefs; beyond it, only those hypotheses which serve for the more accurate asking of questions.

To sum up:—

We may believe what goes beyond our experience, only when it is inferred from that experience by the assumption that what we do not know is like what we know.

We may believe the statement of another person, when there is reasonable ground for supposing that he knows the matter of which he speaks, and that he is speaking the truth so far as he knows it.

It is wrong in all cases to believe on insufficient evidence; and where it is presumption to doubt and to investigate, there it is worse than presumption to believe.

THE ETHICS OF RELIGION [1]

THE word *religion* is used in many different meanings, and there have been not a few controversies in which the main difference between the contending parties was only this, that they understood by *religion* two different things. I will therefore begin by setting forth as clearly as I can one or two of the meanings which the word appears to have in popular speech.

First, then, it may mean a body of doctrines, as in the common phrase, " The truth of the Christian religion " ; or in this sentence : " The religion of the Buddha teaches that the soul·is not a distinct substance." Opinions differ upon the question what doctrines may properly be called religious; some people holding that there can be no religion without belief in a God and in a future life, so that in their judgment the body of doctrines must necessarily include these two; while others would insist upon other special dogmas being included, before they could consent to call the system by 'this name. But the number of such people is daily diminishing, by reason of the spread and the increase of our knowledge about distant countries and races. To me, indeed, it would seem rash to assert of any doctrine or its contrary that it might not form part of a religion. But, fortunately, it is not necessary to any part of the discussion on which I propose to enter that this question should be settled.

Secondly, religion may mean a *ceremonial* or *cult*, involving an organised priesthood and a machinery of sacred things and places. In this sense we speak of the clergy as ministers of religion, or of a State as tolerating the practice of certain religions. There is a somewhat wider meaning which it will be convenient to consider together with this one, and as a mere extension of it, namely, that in which religion stands for the influence of a certain priesthood. A religion is sometimes said to have been successful when it has got its priests into

[1] *Fortnightly Review*, July 1877.

power; thus some writers speak of the wonderfully rapid success of Christianity. A nation is said to have embraced a religion when the authorities of that nation have granted privileges to the clergy, have made them as far as possible the leaders of society, and have given them a considerable share in the management of public affairs. So the northern nations of Europe are said to have embraced the Catholic religion at an early date. The reason why it seems to me convenient to take these two meanings together is, that they are both related to the priesthood. Although the priesthood itself is not called religion, so far as I know, yet the word is used for the general influence and professional acts of the priesthood.

Thirdly, religion may mean a body of precepts or code of rules, intended to guide human conduct, as in this sentence of the authorised version of the New Testament: " Pure religion and undefiled before God and the Father is this, to visit the fatherless and widows in their affliction, and to keep himself unspotted from the world " (James i. 27). It is sometimes difficult to draw the line between this meaning and the last, for it is a mark of the great majority of religions that they confound ceremonial observances with duties having real moral obligation. Thus in the Jewish decalogue the command to do no work on Saturdays is found side by side with the prohibition of murder and theft. It might seem to be the more correct as well as the more philosophical course to follow in this matter the distinction made by Butler between *moral* and *positive* commands, and to class all those precepts which are not of universal moral obligation under the head of ceremonial. And, in fact, when we come to examine the matter from the point of view of morality, the distinction is of the utmost importance. But from the point of view of religion there are difficulties in making it. In the first place, the distinction is not made, or is not understood, by religious folk in general. Innumerable tracts and pretty stories impress upon us that Sabbath-breaking is rather worse than stealing, and leads naturally on to materialism and murder. Less than a hundred years ago sacrilege was punishable by burning in France, and murder by simple decapitation. In the next place, if we pick out a religion at haphazard, we shall find that it is not at all easy to divide its precepts into those which are really of moral obligation and those which are indifferent and of a ceremonial character. We may find precepts unconnected with any ceremonial, and yet positively immoral; and ceremonials may be immoral in themselves, or constructively immoral on account of their known symbolism. On the whole, it seems to me most convenient to draw the plain and obvious distinction between those actions which a religion prescribes to *all* its followers, whether the actions are ceremonial or not, and those which are prescribed only as professional actions of a sacerdotal class. The latter will come under what I have called the second meaning of religion, the professional acts and the influence of a priesthood. In the third meaning will be included all that practically guides the life of a layman, in so far as this guidance is supplied to him by his religion.

Fourthly, and lastly, there is a meaning of the word *religion* which has been coming more and more prominently forward of late years, till it has even threatened to supersede all the others. Religion has been defined as *morality touched with emotion*. I will not here adopt this definition, because I wish to deal with the concrete in the first place, and only to pass on to the abstract in so far as that previous study appears to lead to it. I wish to consider the facts of religion as we find them, and not ideal possibilities. " Yes, but," every one will say, " if you mean my own religion, it is already, as a matter of fact, morality touched with emotion. It is the highest morality touched with the purest emotion, an emotion directed towards the most worthy of objects." Unfortunately we do not mean your religion alone, but all manner of heresies and heathenisms along with it : the religions of the Thug, of the Jesuit, of the South Sea cannibal, of Confucius, of the poor Indian with his untutored mind, of the Peculiar People, of the Mormons, and of the old cat-worshipping Egyptian. It must be

clear that we shall restrict ourselves to a very narrow
circle of what are commonly called religious facts, unless
we include in our considerations not only morality
touched with emotion, but also immorality touched with
emotion.   In fact, what is really touched with emotion
in any case is that body of precepts for the guidance of a
layman's life which we have taken to be the third meaning
of religion.   In that collection of precepts there may be
some agreeable to morality, and some repugnant to it,
and some indifferent, but being all enjoined by the religion
they will be all touched by the same religious emotion.
Shall we then say that religion means a feeling, an
emotion, an habitual attitude of mind towards some
object or objects, or towards life in general, which has a
bearing upon the way in which men regard the rules of
conduct?   I think the last phrase should be left out.
An habitual attitude of mind, of a religious character,
does always have some bearing upon the way in which
men regard the rules of conduct; but it seems sometimes
as if this were an accident, and not the essence of the
religious feeling.   Some devout people prefer to have
their devotion pure and simple, without admixture of
any such application—they do not want to listen to
" cauld morality."   And it seems as if the religious
feeling of the Greeks, and partly also of our own ancestors, was so far divorced from morality that it affected
it only, as it were, by a side-wind, through the influence
of the character and example of the Gods.   So that it
seems only likely to create confusion if we mix up
morality with this fourth meaning of religion.   Sometimes religion means a code of precepts, and sometimes
it means a devotional habit of mind ; the two things are
sometimes connected, but also they are sometimes quite
distinct.   But that the connection of these two things is
more and more insisted on, that it is the keynote of the
apparent revival of religion which has taken place in this
century, is a very significant fact, about which there is
more to be said.

As to the nature of this devotional habit of mind, there
are no doubt many who would like a closer definition.

But I am not at all prepared to say what attitude of mind may properly be called religious, and what may not. Some will hold that religion must have a person for its object; but the Buddha was filled with religious feeling, and yet he had no personal object. Spinoza, the God-intoxicated man, had no personal object for his devotion. It might be possible to frame a definition which would fairly include all cases, but it would require the expenditure of vast ingenuity and research, and would not, I am inclined to think, be of much use when it was obtained.

Nor is the difficulty to be got over by taking any definite and well-organised sect, whose principles are settled in black and white; for example, the Roman Catholic Church, whose seamless unity has just been exhibited and protected by an Œcumenical Council. Shall we listen to Mr. Mivart, who " execrates without reserve Marian persecutions, the Massacre of St. Bartholomew, and all similar acts "? or to the editor of the *Dublin Review*, who thinks that a teacher of false doctrines " should be visited by the law with just that amount of severity which the public sentiment will bear "? For assuredly common-sense morality will pass very different judgments on these two distinct religions, although it appears that experts have found room for both of them within the limits of the Vatican definitions.

Moreover, there is very great good to be got by widening our view of what may be contained in religion. If we go to a man and propose to test his own religion by the canons of common-sense morality, he will be, most likely, offended, for he will say that his religion is far too sublime and exalted to be affected by considerations of that sort. But he will have no such objection in the case of other people's religion. And when he has found that in the name of religion other people, in other circumstances, have believed in doctrines that were false, have supported priesthoods that were social evils, have taken wrong for right, and have even poisoned the very sources of morality, he may be tempted to ask himself, " Is there no trace of any of these evils in my own religion, or at least in my own conception and practice of

it?" And that is just what we want him to do. Bring
your doctrines, your priesthoods, your precepts, yea, even
the inner devotion of your soul, before the tribunal of
conscience; she is no man's and no God's vicar, but the
supreme judge of men and Gods.

Let us inquire, then, what morality has to say in regard
to religious doctrines. It deals with the *manner* of
religious belief directly, and with the *matter* indirectly.
Religious beliefs must be founded on evidence; if they
are not so founded, it is wrong to hold them. The rule
of right conduct in this matter is exactly the opposite of
that implied in the two famous texts : " He that believeth
not shall be damned," and " Blessed are they that have
not seen and yet have believed." For a man who clearly
felt and recognised the duty of intellectual honesty, of
carefully testing every belief before he received it, and
especially before he recommended it to others, it would
be impossible to ascribe the profoundly immoral teaching
of these texts to a true prophet or worthy leader of
humanity. It will comfort those who wish to preserve
their reverence for the character of a great teacher to
remember that one of these sayings is in the well-known
forged passage at the end of the second gospel, and that
the other occurs only in the late and legendary fourth
gospel; both being described as spoken under utterly
impossible circumstances. These precepts belong to the
Church and not to the Gospel. But whoever wrote
either of them down as a deliverance of one whom he
supposed to be a divine teacher, has thereby written
down himself as a man void of intellectual honesty, as a
man whose word cannot be trusted, as a man who would
accept and spread about any kind of baseless fiction for
fear of believing too little.

So far as to the manner of religious belief. Let us
now inquire what bearing morality has upon its matter.
We may see at once that this can only be indirect ; for
the rightness or wrongness of belief in a doctrine depends
only upon the nature of the evidence for it, and not upon
what the doctrine is. But there is a very important way
in which religious doctrine may lead to morality or

immorality, and in which, therefore, morality has a bearing upon doctrine. It is when that doctrine declares the character and actions of the Gods who are regarded as objects of reverence and worship. If a God is represented as doing that which is clearly wrong, and it still held up to the reverence of men, they will be tempted to think that in doing this wrong thing they are not so very wrong after all, but are only following an example which all men respect. So says Plato [1]:—

" We must not tell a youthful listener that he will be doing nothing extraordinary if he commit the foulest crimes, nor yet if he chastise the crimes of a father in the most unscrupulous manner, but will simply be doing what the first and greatest of the Gods have done before him. . . .

" Nor yet is it proper to say in any case—what is indeed untrue—that Gods wage war against Gods, and intrigue and fight among themselves; that is, if the future guardians of our state are to deem it a most disgraceful thing to quarrel lightly with one another: far less ought we to select as subjects for fiction and embroidery the battles of the giants, and numerous other feuds of all sorts, in which Gods and heroes fight against their own kith and kin. But if there is any possibility of persuading them that to quarrel with one's fellow is a sin of which no member of a state was ever guilty, such ought rather to be the language held to our children from the first, by old men and old women, and all elderly persons; and such is the strain in which our poets must be compelled to write. But stories like the chaining of Hera by her son, and the flinging of Hephaistos out of heaven for trying to take his mother's part when his father was beating her, and all those battles of the Gods which are to be found in Homer, must be refused admittance into our state, whether they be allegorical or not. For a child cannot discriminate between what is allegory and what is not; and whatever at that age is adopted as a matter of belief has a tendency to become

[1] *Rep.* ii. 378. Tr. Davies and Vaughan.

fixed and indelible, and therefore, perhaps, we ought to esteem it of the greatest importance that the fictions which children first hear should be adapted in the most perfect manner to the promotion of virtue."

And Seneca says the same thing, with still more reason in his day and country : " What else is this appeal to the precedent of the Gods for, but to inflame our lusts, and to furnish licence and excuse for the corrupt act under the divine protection? " And again, of the character of Jupiter as described in the popular legends: " This has led to no other result than to deprive sin of its shame in man's eyes, by showing him the God no better than himself." In Imperial Rome, the sink of all nations, it was not uncommon to find " the intending sinner addressing to the deified vice which he contemplated a prayer for the success of his design; the adulteress imploring of Venus the favours of her paramour; . . . the thief praying to Hermes Dolios for aid in his enter-prise, or offering up to him the first fruits of his plunder; . . . youths entreating Hercules to expedite the death of a rich uncle." [1]

When we reflect that criminal deities were worshipped all over the empire, we cannot but wonder that any good people were left; that man could still be holy, although every God was vile. Yet this was undoubtedly the case; the social forces worked steadily on wherever there was peace and a settled government and municipal freedom; and the wicked stories of theologians were somehow explained away and disregarded. If men were no better than their religions, the world would be a hell indeed.

It is very important, however, to consider what really ought to be done in the case of stories like these. When the poet sings that Zeus kicked Hephaistos out of heaven for trying to help his mother, Plato says that this fiction must be suppressed by law. We cannot follow him there, for since his time we have had too much of trying to suppress false doctrines by law. Plato thinks it quite obviously clear that God cannot produce evil, and he

[1] *North British Review*, 1867, p. 284.

would stop everybody's mouth who ventured to say that he can. But in regard to the doctrine itself, we can only ask, " Is it true? " And that is a question to be settled by evidence. Did Zeus commit this crime, or did he not? We must ask the apologists, the reconcilers of religion and science, what evidence they can produce to prove that Zeus kicked Hephaistos out of heaven. That a doctrine may lead to immoral consequences is no reason for disbelieving it. But whether the doctrine were true or false, one thing does clearly follow from its moral character : namely this, that if Zeus behaved as he is said to have behaved, he ought not to be worshipped. To those who complain of his violence and injustice, it is no answer to say that the divine attributes are far above human comprehension; that the ways of Zeus are not our ways, neither are his thoughts our thoughts. If he is to be worshipped, he must do something vaster and nobler and greater than good men do, but it must be like what they do in its goodness. His actions must not be merely a magnified copy of what bad men do. So soon as they are thus represented, morality has something to say. Not indeed about the fact; for it is not conscience, but reason, that has to judge matters of fact; but about the worship of a character so represented. If there really is good evidence that Zeus kicked Hephaistos out of heaven, and seduced Alkmene by a mean trick, say so by all means; but say also that it is wrong to salute his priests or to make offerings in his temple.

When men do their duty in this respect, morality has a very curious indirect effect on the religious doctrine itself. As soon as the offerings become less frequent, the evidence for the doctrine begins to fade away; the process of theological interpretation gradually brings out the true inner meaning of it, that Zeus did not kick Hephaistos out of heaven, and did not seduce Alkmene.

Is this a merely theoretical discussion about far-away things? Let us come back for a moment to our own time and country, and think whether there can be any lesson for us in this refusal of common-sense morality to worship a deity whose actions are a magnified copy of

what bad men do.   There are three doctrines which find
very wide acceptance among our countrymen at the
present day : the doctrines of original sin, of a vicarious
sacrifice, and of eternal punishments.   We are not
concerned with any refined evaporations of these doctrines which are exhaled by courtly theologians, but with
the naked statements which are put into the minds of
children and of ignorant people, which are taught broad-
cast and without shame in denominational schools.
Father Faber, good soul, persuaded himself that after all
only a very few people would be really damned, and
Father Oxenham gives one the impression that it will not
hurt even them very much.   But one learns the practical
teaching of the Church from such books as *A Glimpse of
Hell*, where a child is described as thrown between the
bars upon the burning coals, there to writhe for ever.
The masses do not get the elegant emasculations of
Father Faber and Father Oxenham; they get " a
Glimpse of Hell."

Now to condemn all mankind for the sin of Adam and
Eve; to let the innocent suffer for the guilty; to keep
anyone alive in torture for ever and ever; these actions
are simply magnified copies of what bad men do.   No
juggling with " divine justice and mercy " can make
them anything else.   This must be said to all kinds and
conditions of men :   that if God holds all mankind
guilty for the sin of Adam, if he has visited upon the
innocent the punishment of the guilty, if he is to torture
any single soul for ever, then it is wrong to worship him.

But there is something to be said also to those who
think that religious beliefs are not indeed true, but are
useful for the masses; who deprecate any open and
public argument against them, and think that all
sceptical books should be published at a high price; who
go to church, not because they approve of it themselves,
but to set an example to the servants.   Let us ask them
to ponder the words of Plato, who, like them, thought
that all these tales of the Gods were fables, but still fables
which might be useful to amuse children with: " *We
ought to esteem it of the greatest importance that the*

fictions which children first hear should be adapted in the most perfect manner to the promotion of virtue." If we grant to you that it is good for poor people and children to believe some of these fictions, is it not better, at least, that they should believe those which are adapted to the promotion of virtue? Now the stories which you send your servants and children to hear are adapted to the promotion of vice. So far as the remedy is in your own hands, you are bound to apply it; stop your voluntary subscriptions and the moral support of your presence from any place where the criminal doctrines are taught. You will find more men and better men to preach that which is agreeable to their conscience, than to thunder out doctrines under which their minds are always uneasy, and which only a continual self-deception can keep them from feeling to be wicked.

Let us now go on to inquire what morality has to say in the matter of religious *ministrations,* the official acts and the general influence of a priesthood. This question seems to me a more difficult one than the former; at any rate it is not so easy to find general principles which are at once simple in their nature and clear to the conscience of any man who honestly considers them. One such principle, indeed, there is, which can hardly be stated in a Protestant country without meeting with a cordial response: being indeed that characteristic of our race which made the Reformation a necessity, and became the soul of the Protestant movement. I mean the principle which forbids the priest to come between a man and his conscience. If it be true, as our daily experience teaches us, that the moral sense gains in clearness and power by exercise, by the constant endeavour to find out and to see for ourselves what is right and what is wrong, it must be nothing short of a moral suicide to delegate our conscience to another man. It is true that when we are in difficulties and do not altogether see our way, we quite rightly seek counsel and advice of some friend who has more experience, more wisdom begot by it, more devotion to the right than ourselves, and who not being involved in the difficulties which encompass us, may more easily see the way out of them. But such counsel does not and ought not to take the place of our private judgment; on the contrary, among wise men it is asked and given for the purpose of helping and supporting private judgment. I should go to my friend, not that he may tell me what to do, but that he may help me to see what is right.

Now, as we all know, there is a priesthood whose influence is not to be made light of, even in our own land, which claims to do two things : to declare with infallible authority what is right and what is wrong, and to take away the guilt of the sinner after confession has been made to it. The second of these claims we shall come back upon in connection with another part of the subject. But that claim is one which, as it seems to me, ought to condemn the priesthood making it in the eyes of every conscientious man. We must take care to keep this question to itself, and not to let it be confused with quite different ones. The priesthood in question, as we all know, has taught that as right which is not right, and has condemned as wrong some of the holiest duties of mankind. But this is not what we are here concerned with. Let us put an ideal case of a priesthood which, as a matter of fact, taught a morality agreeing with the healthy conscience of all men at a given time; but which, nevertheless, taught this as an infallible revelation. The tendency of such teaching, if really accepted, would be to destroy morality altogether, for it is of the very essence of the moral sense that it is a common perception by men of what is good for man. It arises, not in one man's mind by a flash of genius or a transport ecstasy, but in all men's minds, as the fruit of their necessary intercourse and united labour for a common object. When an infallible authority is set up, the voice of this natural human conscience must be hushed and schooled, and made to speak the words of a formula. Obedience becomes the whole duty of man; and the notion of right is attached to a lifeless code of rules, instead of being the informing character of a nation. The natural consequence is that it fades gradually out and ends by disappearing altogether. I am not describing a purely conjectural state of things, but an effect which has actually been produced at various times and in considerable populations by the influence of the Catholic Church. It is true that we cannot find an actually crucial instance of a pure morality taught as an infallible revelation, and so in time ceasing to be morality for that reason alone. There are two circumstances which prevent this. One is that the Catholic priesthood has always practically taught an imperfect morality, and that it is difficult to distinguish between the effects of precepts which are wrong in themselves, and precepts which are only wrong because of the manner in which they are enforced. The other circumstance is that the priesthood has very rarely found a population willing to place itself completely and absolutely under priestly control. Men must live together and work for common objects even in priest-ridden countries; and those conditions which in the course of ages have been able to create the moral sense cannot fail in some degree to recall it to men's minds and gradually to reinforce it. Thus it comes about that a great and increasing portion of life breaks free from priestly influences, and is governed upon right and rational grounds. The goodness of men shows itself in time more powerful than the wickedness of some of their religions.

The practical inference is, then, that we ought to do all in our power to restrain and diminish the influence of any priesthood which claims to rule consciences. But when we attempt to go beyond this plain Protestant principle, we find that the question is one of history and politics. The question which we want to ask ourselves— " Is it right to support this or that priesthood? "— can only be answered by this other question, " What has it done or got done? "

In asking this question, we must bear in mind that the word *priesthood*, as we have used it hitherto, has a very wide meaning—namely, it means any body of men who perform special ceremonies in the name of religion; a *ceremony* being an act which is prescribed by religion to that body of men, but not on account of its intrinsic rightness or wrongness. It includes, therefore, not only the priests of Catholicism, or of the Obi rites, who lay claim to a magical character and powers, but more familiar clergymen or ministers of Protestant denominations, and the members of monastic orders. But there is a considerable difference, pointed out by Hume, between a priest who lays claim to a magical character and powers, and a clergyman, in the English sense, as it was understood in Hume's day, whose office was to remind people of their duties every Sunday, and to represent a certain standard of culture in remote country districts. It will, perhaps, conduce to clearness if we use the word *priest* exclusively in the first sense.

There is another confusion which we must endeavour to avoid, if we would really get at the truth of this matter. When one ventures to doubt whether the Catholic clergy has really been an unmixed blessing to Europe, one is generally met by the reply, " You cannot find any fault with the Sermon on the Mount." Now it would be too much to say that this has nothing to do with the question we are proposing to ask, for there is a sense in which the Sermon on the Mount and the Catholic clergy have something to do with each other. The Sermon on the Mount is admitted on all hands to be the best and most precious thing that Christianity has offered to the world; and it cannot be doubted that the Catholic clergy of East and West were the only spokesmen of Christianity until the Reformation, and are the spokesmen of the vast majority of Christians at this moment. But it must surely be unnecessary to say in a Protestant country that the Catholic Church and the Gospel are two very different things. The moral teaching of Christ, as partly preserved in the three first gospels, or—which is the same thing—the moral teaching of the great Rabbi Hillel, as partly preserved in the Pirkè Aboth, is the expression of the conscience of a people who had fought long and heroically for their national existence. In that terrible conflict they had learned the supreme and overwhelming importance of conduct, the necessity for those who would survive of fighting manfully for their lives and making a stand against the hostile powers around; the weakness and uselessness of solitary and selfish efforts, the necessity for a man who would be a man to lose his poor single personality in the being of a greater and nobler combatant—the nation. And they said all this, after their fashion of short and potent sayings, perhaps better than any other men have said it before or since. " If I am not for myself," said the great Hillel, " who is for me? And if I am only for myself, where is the use of me? *And if not now, when?*" It would be hard to find a more striking contrast than exists between the sturdy unselfish independence of this saying, and the abject and selfish servility of the priest-ridden claimant of the skies. It was this heroic people that produced the morality of the Sermon on the Mount. But it was not they who produced the priests and the dogmas of Catholicism. Shaven crowns, linen vestments, and the claim to priestly rule over consciences, these were dwellers on the banks of the Nile. The Gospel indeed came out of Judæa, but the Church and her dogmas came out of Egypt. Not, as it is written, " Out of Egypt have I called my son," but, " Out of Egypt have I called my daughter." St. Gregory of Nazianzum remarked with wonder that Egypt, having so lately worshipped bulls, goats, and crocodiles, was now teaching the world the worship of the Trinity in its truest form.[1] Poor, simple St. Gregory! it was not that Egypt had risen higher, but that the world had sunk lower. The empire, which in the time of Augustus had dreaded, and with reason, the corrupting influence of Egyptian superstitions, was now eaten up by them, and rapidly rotting away.

Then, when we ask what has been the influence of the Catholic clergy upon European nations, we are not inquiring about the results of accepting the morality of the Sermon on the Mount; we are inquiring into the effect of attaching an Egyptian priesthood, which teaches Egyptian dogmas, to the life and sayings of a Jewish prophet.

[1] See Sharpe, *Egyptian Mythology and Egyptian Christianity,* p. 114.

In this inquiry, which requires the knowledge of facts beyond our own immediate experience, we must make use of the great principle of authority, which enables us to profit by the experience of other men. The great civilised countries on the continent of Europe at the present day— France, Germany, Austria, and Italy—have had an extensive experience of the Catholic clergy for a great number of centuries, and they are forced by strong practical reasons to form a judgment upon the character and tendencies of an institution which is sufficiently powerful to command the attention of all who are interested in public affairs. We might add the experience of our forefathers three centuries ago, and of Ireland at this moment; but home politics are apt to be looked upon with other eyes than those of reason. Let us hear, then, the judgment of the civilised people of Europe on this question.

It is a matter of notoriety that an aider and abettor of clerical pretensions is regarded in France as an enemy of France and of Frenchmen; in Germany as an enemy of Germany and of Germans; in Austria as an enemy of Austria and Hungary, of both Austrians and Magyars; and in Italy as an enemy to Italy and the Italians. He is so regarded, not by a few wild and revolutionary enthusiasts who have cast away all the beliefs of their childhood and all bonds connecting them with the past, but by a great and increasing majority of sober and conscientious men of all creeds and persuasions, who are filled with a love for their country, and whose hopes and aims for the future are animated and guided by the examples of those who have gone before them, and by a sense of the continuity of national life. The profound conviction and determination of the people in all these countries, that the clergy must be restricted to a purely ceremonial province, and must not be allowed to interfere, as clergy, in public affairs—this conviction and determination, I say, are not the effect of a rejection of the Catholic dogmas. Such rejection has not in fact been made in Catholic countries by the great majority. It involves many difficult speculative questions, the profound disturbance of old habits of thought, and the toilsome consideration of abstract ideas. But such is the happy inconsistency of human nature, that men who would be shocked and pained by a doubt about the central doctrines of their religions are far more really and practically shocked and pained by the moral consequences of clerical ascendency. About the dogmas they do not know; they were taught them in childhood, and have not inquired into them since, and therefore they are not competent witnesses to the truth of them. But about the priesthood they do know, by daily and hourly experience; and to its character they are competent witnesses. No· man can express his convictions more forcibly than by acting upon them in a great and solemn matter of national importance. In all these countries the conviction of the serious and sober majority of the people is embodied, and is being daily embodied, in special legislation, openly and avowedly intended to guard against clerical aggression. The more closely the legislature of these countries reflects the popular will, the more clear and pronounced does this tendency become. It may be thwarted or evaded for the moment by constitutional devices and parliamentary tricks, but sooner or later the nation will be thoroughly represented in all of them: and as to what is then to be expected, let the panic of the clerical parties make answer.

This is a state of opinion and of feeling which we in our own country find it hard to understand, although it is one of the most persistent characters of our nation in past times. We have spoken so plainly and struck so hard in the past, that we seem to have won the right to let this matter alone. We think our enemies are dead, and we forget that our neighbour's enemies are plainly alive: and then we wonder that he does not sit down and be quiet as we are. We are not much accustomed to be afraid, and we never know when we are beaten. But those who are nearer to the danger feel a very real and, it seems to me, well-grounded fear. The whole structure of modern society, the fruit of long and painful efforts, the hopes of further improvement, the triumphs of justice, of freedom, and of light, the bonds of patriotism which make each nation one, the bonds of humanity which bring different nations together—all these they see to be menaced with a great and real and even pressing danger. For myself I confess that I cannot help feeling as they feel. It seems to me quite possible that the moral and intellectual culture of Europe, the light and the right, what makes life worth having and men worthy to have it, may be clean swept away by a revival of superstition. We are, perhaps, ourselves not free from such a domestic danger; but no one can doubt that the danger would speedily arise if all Europe at our side should become again barbaric, not with the weakness and docility of a barbarism which has never known better, but with the strength of a past civilisation perverted to the service of evil.

Those who know best, then, about the Catholic priesthood at present, regard it as a standing menace to the state and to the moral fabric of society.

Some would have us believe that this condition of things is quite new, and has in fact been created by the Vatican Council. In the Middle Ages, they say, the Church did incalculable service; or even if you do not allow that, yet the ancient Egyptian priesthood invented many useful arts; or if you have read anything which is not to their credit, there were the Babylonians and Assyrians who had priests thousands of years ago; and in fact the more you go back into prehistoric ages, and the farther you go away into distant countries, the less you can find to say against the priesthoods of those times and places. This statement, for which there is certainly much foundation, may be put into another form: the more you come forward into modern times and neighbouring countries, where the facts can actually be got at, the more complete is the evidence against the priesthoods of these times and places. But the whole argument is founded upon what is at least a doubtful view of human nature and of society. Just as an early school of geologists were accustomed to explain the present state of the earth's surface by supposing that in primitive ages the processes of geologic change were far more violent and rapid than they are now—so catastrophic, indeed, as to constitute a thoroughly different state of things—so there is a school of historians who think that the intimate structure of human nature, its capabilities of learning and of adapting itself to society, have so far altered within the historic period as to make the present processes of social change totally different in character from those even of the moderately distant past. They think that institutions and conditions which are plainly harmful to us now have at other times and places done good and serviceable work. War, pestilence, priestcraft, and slavery have been represented as positive boons to an early state of society. They are not blessings to us, it is true; but then times have altered very much.

On the other hand, a later school of geologists have seen reason to think that the processes of change have never, since the earth finally solidified, been very different from what they are now. More rapid, indeed, they must have been in early times, for many reasons ; but not so very much more rapid as to constitute an entirely different state of things. And it does seem to me in like manner that a wider and more rational view of history will recognise more and more of the permanent, and less and less of the changeable, element in human nature. No doubt our ancestors of a thousand generations back were very different beings from ourselves ; perhaps fifty thousand generations back they were not men at all. But the historic period is hardly to be stretched beyond two hundred generations; and it seems unreasonable to expect that in such a tiny page of our biography we can trace with clearness the growth and progress of a long life. Compare Egypt in the time of King Menes, say six thousand years ago, with Spain in this present century, before Englishmen made any railways there: I suppose the main difference is that the Egyptians washed themselves. It seems more analogous to what we find in other fields of inquiry to suppose that there are certain great broad principles of human life which have been true all along ; that certain conditions have always been favourable to the health of society, and certain other conditions always hurtful.

Now, although I have many times asked for it from those who said that somewhere and at some time mankind had derived benefits from a priesthood laying claim to a magical character and powers, I have never been able to get any evidence for their statement. Nobody will give me a date, and a latitude and longitude, that I may examine into the matter. " In the Middle Ages the priests and monks were the sole depositaries of learning." Quite so ; a man burns your house to the ground, builds a wretched hovel on the ruins, and then takes credit for whatever shelter there is about the place. In the Middle Ages nearly all learned men were obliged to become priests and monks. " Then again, the bishops have sometimes acted as tribunes of the people, to protect them against the tyranny of kings." No doubt, when Pope and Cæsar fall out, honest men may come by their own. If two men rob you in a dark lane, and then quarrel over the plunder, so that you get a chance to escape with your life, you will of course be very grateful to each of them for having prevented the other from killing you; but you would be much more grateful to a policeman who locked them both up. Two powers have sought to enslave the people, and have quarrelled with each other; certainly we are very much obliged to them for quarrelling, but a condition of still greater happiness and security would be the non-existence of both.

I can find no evidence that seriously militates against the rule that the priest is at all times and in all places the enemy of all men—*Sacerdos semper, ubique, et omnibus inimicus.* I do not deny that the priest is very often a most earnest and conscientious man, doing the very best that he knows of as well as he can do it. Lord Amberley is quite right in saying that the blame rests more with the laity than with the priesthood; that it has insisted on magic and mysteries, and has forced the priesthood to produce them. But then, how dreadful is the system that puts good men to such uses!

And although it is true that in its origin a priesthood is

the effect of an evil already existing, a symptom of social disease rather than a cause of it, yet, once being created and made powerful, it tends in many ways to prolong and increase the disease which gave it birth. One of these ways is so marked and of such practical importance that we are bound to consider it here; I mean the education of children. If there is one lesson which history forces upon us in every page, it is this: *Keep your children away from the priest, or he will make them the enemies of mankind.* It is not the Catholic clergy and those like them who are alone to be dreaded in this matter; even the representatives of apparently harmless religions may do incalculable mischief if they get education into their hands. To the early Mohammedans the mosque was the one public building in every place where public business could be transacted; and so it was naturally the place of primary education, which they held to be a matter of supreme importance. By and by, as the clergy grew up, the mosque was gradually usurped by them, and primary education fell into their hands. Then ensued a " revival of religion "; religion became a fanaticism: books were burnt and universities were closed; the empire rotted away in East and West, until it was conquered by Turkish savages in Asia and by Christian savages in Spain.

The labours of students of the early history of institutions—notably Sir Henry Maine and M. de Laveleye—have disclosed us an element of society which appears to have existed in all times and places, and which is the basis of our own social structure. The village community, or commune, or township, found in tribes of the most varied race and time, has so modified itself as to get adapted in one place or another to all the different conditions of human existence. This union of men to work for a common object has transformed them from wild animals into tame ones. Century by century the educating process of the social life has been working at human nature; it has built itself into our inmost soul. Such as we are—moral and rational beings—thinking and talking in general conceptions about the facts that make up our life, feeling a necessity to act, not for ourselves, but for Ourself, for the larger life of Man in which we are elements; such moral and rational beings, I say, Man has made us. By Man I mean men organised into a society, which fights for its life, not only as a mere collection of men who must separately be kept alive, but as a society. It must fight, not only against external enemies, but against treason and disruption within it. Hence comes the unity of interest of all its members; each of them has to feel that he is not himself only but a part of all the rest. Conscience—the sense of right and wrong—springs out of the habit of judging things from the point of view of all and not of one. It is Ourself, not ourselves, that makes for righteousness.

The codes of morality, then, which are adopted into various religions, and afterwards taught as parts of religious systems, are derived from secular sources. The most ancient version of the Ten Commandments, whatever the investigations of scholars may make it out to be, originates, not in the thunders of Sinai, but in the peaceful life of men on the plains of Chaldæa. Conscience is the voice of Man ingrained into our hearts, commanding us to work for Man.

Religions differ in the treatment which they give to this most sacred heirloom of our past history. Sometimes they invert its precepts—telling men to be submissive under oppression because the powers that be are ordained of God; telling them to believe where they have not seen, and to play with falsehood in order that a particular doctrine may prevail, instead of seeking for truth whatever it may be; telling them to betray their country for the sake of their Church. But there is one great distinction to which I wish, in conclusion, to call special attention—a distinction between two kinds of religious emotion which bear upon the conduct of men.

We said that conscience is the voice of Man within us, commanding us to work for Man. We do not know this immediately by our own experience; we only know that something within us commands us to work for Man. This fact men have tried to explain; and they have thought, for the most part, that this voice was the voice of a God.   But the explanation takes two different forms: the God may speak in us for Man's sake, or for his own sake.   If he speaks for his own sake—and this is what generally happens when he has priests who lay claim to a magical character and powers—our allegiance is apt to be taken away from Man, and transferred to the God. When we love our brother for the sake of our brother, we help all men to grow in the right; but when we love our brother for the sake of somebody else, who is very likely to damn our brother, it very soon comes to burning him alive for his soul's health.   When men respect human life for the sake of Man, tranquillity, order, and progress go hand in hand; but those who only respected human life because God had forbidden murder have set their mark upon Europe in fifteen centuries of blood and fire.

These are only two examples of a general rule.   Wherever the allegiance of men has been diverted from Man to some divinity who speaks to men for his own sake and seeks his own glory, one thing has happened.   The right precepts might be enforced, but they were enforced upon wrong grounds, and they were not obeyed.   But right precepts are not always enforced; the fact that the fountains of morality have been poisoned makes it easy to substitute wrong precepts for right ones.

To this same treason against humanity belongs the claim of the priesthood to take away the guilt of a sinner after confession has been made of it.   The Catholic priest professes to act as an ambassador for his God, and to absolve the guilty man by conveying to him the forgiveness of heaven.   If his credentials were ever so sure, if he were indeed the ambassador of a superhuman power, the claim would be treasonable.   Can the favour of the Czar make guiltless the murderer of old men and women and children in Circassian valleys?   Can the pardon of the Sultan make clean the bloody hands of a Pasha?   As little can any God forgive sins committed against man.   When men think he can, they compound for old sins which the God did not like by committing new ones which he does like.   Many a remorseful despot has atoned for the levities of his youth by the persecution of heretics in his old age. That frightful crime, the adulteration of food, could not possibly be so common amongst us if men were not taught to regard it as merely objectionable because it is remotely connected with stealing, of which God has expressed his disapproval in the Decalogue; and therefore as quite naturally set right by a punctual attendance at church on Sundays. When a Ritualist breaks his fast before celebrating the Holy Communion, his deity can forgive him if he likes, for the matter concerns nobody else; but no deity can forgive him for preventing his parishioners from setting up a public library and reading-room for fear they should read Mr. Darwin's works in it. That sin is committed against the people, and a God cannot take it away.

I call those religions which undermine the supreme allegiance of the conscience to Man *ultramontane* religions, because they seek their springs of action *ultra montes*, outside of the common experience and daily life of man. And I remark about them that they are especially apt to teach wrong precepts, and that even when they command men to do the right things they put the command upon wrong motives, and do not get the things done.

But there are forms of religious emotion which do not thus undermine the conscience. Far be it from me to undervalue the help and strength which many of the bravest of our brethren have drawn from the thought of an unseen helper of men. He who, wearied or stricken in the fight with the powers of darkness, asks himself in a solitary place, "Is it all for nothing? shall we indeed be overthrown?"—he does find something which may justify that thought. In such a moment of utter sincerity, when a man has bared his own soul before the immensities and the eternities, a presence in which his own poor personality is shrivelled into nothingness arises within him, and says, as plainly as words can say, "I am with thee, and I am greater than thou." Many names of Gods, of many shapes, have men given to this presence; seeking by names and pictures to know more clearly and

to remember more continually the guide and the helper
of men. No such comradeship with the Great Companion shall have anything but reverence from me, who
have known the divine gentleness of Denison Maurice,
the strong and healthy practical instinct of Charles
Kingsley, and who now revere with all my heart the
teaching of James Martineau. They seem to me, one
and all, to be reaching forward with loving anticipation
to a clearer vision which is yet to come—*tendentesque
manus ripae ulterioris amore*. For, after all, such a
helper of men, outside of humanity, the truth will not
allow us to see. The dim and shadowy outlines of the
superhuman deity fade slowly away from before us; and
as the mist of his presence floats aside, we perceive with
greater and greater clearness the shape of a yet grander
and nobler figure—of Him who made all Gods and shall
unmake them. From the dim dawn of history, and from
the inmost depth of every soul, the face of our father
Man looks out upon us with the fire of eternal youth in
his eyes, and says, " Before Jehovah was, I am! "

THE INFLUENCE UPON MORALITY OF A DECLINE IN RELIGIOUS BELIEF

FROM "A MODERN SYMPOSIUM"

(*In No. 2 of " The Nineteenth Century"*)

IN the third of the preceding discourses [1] there is so much which I can fully and fervently accept, that I should find it far more grateful to rest in that feeling of admiration and sympathy than to attend to points of difference which seem to me to be of altogether secondary import. But for the truth's sake this must first be done, because it will then be more easy to point out some of the bearings of the position held in that discourse upon the question which is under discussion.

That the sense of duty in a man is the prompting of a self other than his own, is the very essence of it. Not only would morals not be self-sufficing, if there were no such prompting of a wider self, but they could not exist : one might as well suppose a fire without heat. Not only is a sense of duty inherent in the constitution of our nature, but the prompting of a wider self than that of the individual is inherent in a sense of duty. It is no more possible to have the right without unselfishness than to have man without a feeling for the right.

We may explain or account for these facts in various ways, but we shall not thereby alter the facts. No theories about heat and light will ever make a cold fire. And no doubt or disproof of any existing theory can any more extinguish that self other than myself, which speaks to me in the voice of conscience, than doubt or disproof of the wave-theory of light can put out the noonday sun.

One such theory is defended in the discourse here dealt with, and, if I may venture to say so, is not quite sufficiently distinguished from the facts which it is meant

[1] By Dr. Martineau.

to explain. The theory is this: that the voice of conscience in my mind is the voice of a conscious being
external to me and to all men, who has made us and all
the world. When this theory is admitted, the observed
discrepancy between our moral sense and the government of the world as a whole makes it necessary to suppose
another world and another life in it for men, whereby
this discord shall be resolved in a final harmony.

I fully admit that the theistic hypothesis, so grounded,
and considered apart from objections otherwise arising,
is a reasonable hypothesis and an explanation of the
facts. The idea of an external conscious being is unavoidably suggested, as it seems to me, by the categorical
imperative of the moral sense; and moreover, in a way
quite independent, by the aspect of nature, which seems
to answer to our questionings with an intelligence akin to
our own. It is more reasonable to assume one consciousness than two, if by that one assumption we can explain
two distinct facts; just as if we had been led to assume an
ether to explain light, and an ether to explain electricity,
we might have run before experiment and guessed that
these two ethers were but one. But since there is a dis-
cordance between nature and conscience, the theory of
their common origin in a mind external to humanity has
not met with such acceptance as that of the divine origin
of each. A large number of theists have rejected it, and
taken refuge in Manichæism and the doctrine of the
Demiurgus in various forms; while others have endeavoured, as aforesaid, to redress the balance of the old
world by calling into existence a new one.

It is, however, a very striking and significant fact that
the great majority of mankind who have thought about
these questions at all, while acknowledging the existence
of divine beings and their influence in the government of
the world, have sought for the spring and sanction of
duty in something above and beyond the Gods. The
religions of Brahmanism and of Buddhism, and the moral
system of Confucius, have together ruled over more than
two-thirds of the human race during the historic period;
and in all of these the moral sense is regarded as arising

indeed out of a universal principle, but not as personified in any conscious being.   This vast body of dissent might well, it should seem, make us ask if there is not something unsatisfying in the theory which represents the voice of conscience as the voice of a God.

Although, as I have said, the idea of an external conscious being is unavoidably suggested by the moral sense, yet, if this idea should be found untrue, it does not follow that nature has been fooling us.   The idea is not in the facts, but in our inference from the facts.   A mirror unavoidably suggests the idea of a room behind it; but it is not our eyes that deceive us, it is only the inference we draw from their testimony.   Further consideration may lead to a different inference of far greater practical value.

Now, whether or no it be reasonable and satisfying to the conscience, it cannot be doubted that theistic belief is a comfort and a solace to those who hold it, and that the loss of it is a very painful loss.   It cannot be doubted, at least, by many of us in this generation, who either profess it now, or received it in our childhood and have parted from it since with such searching trouble as only cradle-faiths can cause.   We have seen the spring sun shine out of an empty heaven, to light up a soulless earth: we have felt with utter loneliness that the Great Companion is dead.   Our children, it may be hoped, will know that sorrow only by the reflex light of a wondering compassion. But to say that theistic belief is a comfort and a solace, and to say that it is the crown or coping of morality, these are different things.

For in what way shall belief in God strengthen my sense of duty?   *He is a great one working for the right.* But I already know so many, and I know these so well. *His righteousness is unfathomable; it transcends all ideals.* But I have not yet fathomed the goodness of living men whom I know; still less of those who have lived, and whom I know.   And the goodness of all these is a striving for something better; now it is not the goal, but the striving for it, that matters to me.   The essence of their goodness is the losing of the individual self in another and a wider self; but God cannot do this; his goodness must be something different. *He is infinitely great and powerful, and he lives for ever.* I do not understand this mensuration of goodness by foot-pounds and seconds and cubic miles. A little field-mouse, which busies itself in the hedge, and does not mind my company, is more to me than the longest ichthyosaurus that ever lived, even if he lived a thousand years. When we look at a starry sky, the spectacle whose awfulness Kant compared with that of the moral sense, does it help out our poetic emotion to reflect that these specks are really very very big, and very very hot, and very very far away? Their heat and their bigness oppress us; we should like them to be taken still farther away, the great blazing lumps. But when we think of the unseen planets that surround them, of the wonders of life, of reason, of love that may dwell therein, then indeed there is something sublime in the sight. Fitness and kinship; these are the truly great things for us, not force and massiveness and length of days.

Length of days, said the old Rabbi, is measured not by their number, but by the work that is done in them. We are all to be swept away in the final ruin of the earth. The thought of that ending is a sad thought; there is no use in trying to deny this. But it has nothing to do with right and wrong; it belongs to another subject. Like All-Father Odin, we must ride out gaily to do battle with the wolf of doom, even if there be no Balder to come back and continue our work. At any rate the right will have been done; and the past is safer than all storehouses.

The conclusion of the matter is that belief in God and in a future life is a source of refined and elevated pleasure to those who can hold it. But the foregoing of a refined and elevated pleasure, because it appears that we have no right to indulge in it, is not in itself, and cannot produce as its consequence, a decline of morality.

There is another theory of the facts of the moral sense set forth in the succeeding discourse,[1] and this seems to me to be the true one. The voice of conscience is the voice of

[1] By Mr. Frederic Harrison.

our Father Man who is within us; the accumulated
instinct of the race is poured into each one of us, and
overflows us, as if the ocean were poured into a cup.[1]
Our evidence for this explanation is that the cause assigned
is a *vera causa*, it undoubtedly exists; there is no
perhaps about that.   And those who have tried tell us
that it is sufficient: the explanation, like the fact,
" covers the whole voluntary field."   The lightest and
the gravest action may be consciously done in and for
Man.   And the sympathetic aspect of nature is explained
to us in the same way.   In so far as our conception of
nature is akin to our minds that conceive it, Man made
it; and Man made us, with the necessity to conceive it in
this way.[2]

I do not, however, suppose that morality would
practically gain much from the wide acceptance of true
views about its nature, except in a way which I shall
presently suggest.   I neither admit the moral influence
of theism in the past, nor look forward to the moral
influence of humanism in the future.   Virtue is a habit,
not a sentiment or an -ism.   The doctrine of total
depravity seems to have been succeeded by a doctrine of
partial depravity, according to which there is hope for
human affairs, but still men cannot go straight unless
some tremendous all-embracing theory has a finger in
the pie.   Theories are most important and excellent
things when they help us to see the matter as it really is,
and so to judge what is the right thing to do in regard to it.
They are the guides of action, but not the springs of it.
Now the spring of virtuous action is the social instinct,
which is to set to work by the practice of comradeship.
The union of men in a common effort for a common
object—*band-work*, if I may venture to translate co-
operation into English—this is and always has been the

----

[1] Schopenhauer.   There is a most remarkable article on the
" Natural History of Morals " in the *North British Review*, December
1867.

[2] For an admirable exposition of the doctrine of the social origin
of our conceptions, see Professor Croom Rovertson's paper, " How
We Come By Our Knowledge," in the first number of the *Nineteenth
Century*.

true school of character. Except in times of severe struggle for national existence, the practice of virtue by masses of men has always been coincident with municipal freedom, and with the vigour of such unions as are not large enough to take from each man his conscious share in the work and in the direction of it.

What really affects morality is not religious belief, but a practice which, in some times and places, is thought to be religious—namely, the practice of submitting human life to clerical control. The apparently destructive tendency of modern times, which arouses fear and the foreboding of evil in the minds of many of the best of men, seems to me to be not mainly an intellectual movement. It has its intellectual side, but that side is the least important, and touches comparatively few souls. The true core of it is a firm resolve of men to know the right at first hand, which has grown out of the strong impulse given to the moral sense by political freedom. Such a resolve is a necessary condition to the existence of a pure and noble theism like that of the third discourse,[1] which learns what God is like by thinking of man's love for man. Although that doctrine has been prefigured and led up to for many ages by the best teaching of Englishmen, and—what is far more important—by the best practice of Englishmen, yet it cannot be accepted on a large scale without what will seem to many a decline of religious belief. For assuredly if men learn the nature of God from the moral sense of man, they cannot go on believing the doctrines of popular theology. Such change of belief is of small account in itself, for any consequences it can bring about; but it is of vast importance as a symptom of the increasing power and clearness of the sense of duty.

On the other hand there is one " decline of religious belief," inseparable from a revolution in human conduct, which would indeed be a frightful disaster to mankind. A revival of any form of sacerdotal Christianity would be a matter of practice and not a matter of theory. The system which sapped the foundations of patriotism in the

[1] Dr. Martineau's.

old world; which well-nigh eradicated the sense of intellectual honesty, and seriously weakened the habit of truth-speaking, which lowered men's reverence for the marriage-bond by placing its sanctions in a realm outside of nature instead of in the common life of men, and by the institutions of monasticism and a celibate clergy; which stunted the moral sense of the nations by putting a priest between every man and his conscience; this system, if it should ever return to power, must be expected to produce worse evils than those which it has worked in the past. The house which it once made desolate has been partially swept and garnished by the free play gained for the natural goodness of men. It would come back accompanied by social diseases perhaps worse than itself, and the wreck of civilised Europe would be darker than the darkest of past ages.

GREAT BOOKS IN PHILOSOPHY PAPERBACK SERIES

ETHICS

Aristotle—*The Nicomachean Ethics*	$8.95
Marcus Aurelius—*Meditations*	5.95
Jeremy Bentham—*The Principles of Morals and Legislation*	8.95
John Dewey—*The Moral Writings of John Dewey, Revised Edition*	
(edited by James Gouinlock)	11.95
Epictetus—*Enchiridion*	4.95
Immanuel Kant—*Fundamental Principles of the Metaphysic of Morals*	5.95
John Stuart Mill—*Utilitarianism*	5.95
George Edward Moore—*Principia Ethica*	8.95
Friedrich Nietzsche—*Beyond Good and Evil*	8.95
Plato—*Protagoras, Philebus,* and *Gorgias*	7.95
Bertrand Russell—*Bertrand Russell On Ethics, Sex, and Marriage*	
(edited by Al Seckel)	19.95
Arthur Schopenhauer—*The Wisdom of Life* and *Counsels and Maxims*	7.95
Benedict de Spinoza—*Ethics* and *The Improvement of the Understanding*	9.95

SOCIAL AND POLITICAL PHILOSOPHY

Aristotle—*The Politics*	7.95
Francis Bacon—*Essays*	6.95
Mikhail Bakunin—*The Basic Bakunin: Writings, 1869–1871*	
(translated and edited by Robert M. Cutler)	11.95
Edmund Burke—*Reflections on the Revolution in France*	7.95
John Dewey—*Freedom and Culture*	10.95
John Dewey—*Individualism Old and New*	9.95
G. W. F. Hegel—*The Philosophy of History*	9.95
G. W. F. Hegel—*Philosophy of Right*	9.95
Thomas Hobbes—*The Leviathan*	7.95
Sidney Hook—*Paradoxes of Freedom*	9.95
Sidney Hook—*Reason, Social Myths, and Democracy*	11.95
John Locke—*Second Treatise on Civil Government*	5.95
Niccolo Machiavelli—*The Prince*	5.95
Karl Marx (with Friedrich Engels)—*The German Ideology,*	
including *Theses on Feuerbach* and *Introduction to the*	
Critique of Political Economy	10.95
Karl Marx—*The Poverty of Philosophy*	7.95
Karl Marx/Friedrich Engels—*The Economic and Philosophic Manuscripts of 1844*	
and *The Communist Manifesto*	6.95
John Stuart Mill—*Considerations on Representative Government*	6.95
John Stuart Mill—*On Liberty*	5.95
John Stuart Mill—*On Socialism*	7.95
John Stuart Mill—*The Subjection of Women*	5.95
Friedrich Nietzsche—*Thus Spake Zarathustra*	9.95
Thomas Paine—*Common Sense*	6.95
Thomas Paine—*Rights of Man*	7.95
Plato—*Lysis, Phaedrus,* and *Symposium*	6.95
Plato—*The Republic*	9.95
Jean-Jacques Rousseau—*The Social Contract*	5.95
Mary Wollstonecraft—*A Vindication of the Rights of Men*	5.95
Mary Wollstonecraft—*A Vindication of the Rights of Women*	6.95

METAPHYSICS/EPISTEMOLOGY

Aristotle—*De Anima*	6.95
Aristotle—*The Metaphysics*	9.95
George Berkeley—*Three Dialogues Between Hylas and Philonous*	5.95
René Descartes—*Discourse on Method* and *The Meditations*	6.95
John Dewey—*How We Think*	10.95
John Dewey—*The Influence of Darwin on Philosophy and Other Essays*	11.95
Epicurus—*The Essential Epicurus: Letters, Principal Doctrines,*	
Vatican Sayings, and Fragments	
(translated, and with an introduction, by Eugene O'Connor)	5.95
Sidney Hook—*The Quest for Being*	11.95
David Hume—*An Enquiry Concerning Human Understanding*	6.95
David Hume—*Treatise of Human Nature*	9.95
William James—*The Meaning of Truth*	11.95
William James—*Pragmatism*	7.95
Immanuel Kant—*Critique of Practical Reason*	7.95
Immanuel Kant—*Critique of Pure Reason*	9.95
Gottfried Wilhelm Leibniz—*Discourse on Method* and the *Monadology*	6.95
John Locke—*An Essay Concerning Human Understanding*	9.95
Charles S. Peirce—*The Essential Writings*	
(edited by Edward C. Moore, preface by Richard Robin)	10.95
Plato—*The Euthyphro, Apology, Crito,* and *Phaedo*	5.95
Bertrand Russell—*The Problems of Philosophy*	8.95
George Santayana—*The Life of Reason*	9.95
Sextus Empiricus—*Outlines of Pyrrhonism*	8.95

PHILOSOPHY OF RELIGION

Marcus Tullius Cicero—*The Nature of the Gods* and *On Divination*	6.95
W. K. Clifford—*The Ethics of Belief and Other Essays*	
(introduction by Timothy J. Madigan)	6.95
Ludwig Feuerbach—*The Essence of Christianity*	8.95
David Hume—*Dialogues Concerning Natural Religion*	5.95
John Locke—*A Letter Concerning Toleration*	5.95
Lucretius—*On the Nature of Things*	7.95
John Stuart Mill—*Three Essays on Religion*	7.95
Thomas Paine—*The Age of Reason*	13.95
Bertrand Russell—*Bertrand Russell On God and Religion* (edited by Al Seckel)	19.95

ESTHETICS

Aristotle—*The Poetics*	5.95
Aristotle—*Treatise on Rhetoric*	7.95

GREAT MINDS PAPERBACK SERIES

ECONOMICS

Charlotte Perkins Gilman—*Women and Economics: A Study of the*	
Economic Relation between Women and Men	11.95
John Maynard Keynes—*The General Theory of Employment, Interest, and Money*	11.95
Thomas R. Malthus—*An Essay on the Principle of Population*	14.95
Alfred Marshall—*Principles of Economics*	11.95
David Ricardo—*Principles of Political Economy and Taxation*	10.95
Adam Smith—*Wealth of Nations*	9.95
Thorstein Veblen—*Theory of the Leisure Class*	11.95

RELIGION

SCIENCE

HISTORY

SOCIOLOGY

CRITICAL ESSAYS

(Prices subject to change without notice.)

ORDER FORM

Prometheus Books
59 John Glenn Drive • Amherst, New York 14228–2197
Telephone: (716) 691–0133

Phone Orders (24 hours):
Toll free (800) 421–0351 • FAX (716) 691–0137
Email: PBooks6205@aol.com

Ship to: _____

Address _____

_____

City _____

County (*N.Y. State Only*) _____

Telephone _____

Prometheus Acct. # _____

❑ Payment enclosed (or)

Charge to ❑ VISA ❑ MasterCard

A/C: ⬜⬜⬜⬜⬜⬜⬜⬜⬜⬜⬜⬜⬜⬜⬜⬜⬜⬜⬜⬜⬜

Exp. Date _____ / _____

Signature _____